PROENSA

Proensa

* * *

An Anthology
of Troubadour Poetry

SELECTED AND TRANSLATED BY

PAUL BLACKBURN

*

EDITED AND INTRODUCED BY

GEORGE ECONOMOU

UNIVERSITY OF CALIFORNIA PRESS
Berkeley • Los Angeles • London

University of California Press
Berkeley and Los Angeles, California

University of California Press, Ltd.
London, England

ISBN 0-520-02985-2
Library of Congress Catalog Card Number: 75-3766

Printed in the United States of America

CONTENTS

v

CONTENTS

CONTENTS

ACKNOWLEDGMENTS

For their help and encouragement, I would like to thank David Antin, Joan Blackburn, Frederick Goldin, and Hugh Kenner.

Robert Creeley, who published the first *Proensa* (Mallorca: Divers Press, 1953), has generously given us permission to use that title again.

Some of these translations have appeared before in various publications: *Anthology of Medieval Lyrics,* ed. Angel Flores (New York: Random House, 1962); *Peire Vidal* (New York/Amherst: Mulch Press, 1972); *Guillem de Poitou* (Mount Horeb, Wisconsin: The Perishable Press, 1976); *Origin,* VI, IX, XI, XII, XV, XVII, XIX, and in *The Gist of "Origin,"* edited by Cid Corman (New York: Grossman, 1976); *Caterpillar,* 10; *Sixpack,* 7/8 (1974), Special Paul Blackburn Issue.

Parts of my discussion of "Ab la dolchor del temps novel" are based on an earlier, considerably different discussion of that poem as a "Test of Translation" for *Caterpillar,* 10 (1970), reprinted in *A Caterpillar Anthology,* ed. Clayton Eshleman (Garden City: Doubleday, 1971).

G. E.

INTRODUCTION

More than any other body of literary work in the western tradition, the poetry of the troubadours has commanded a larger "reputation" than the readership it has actually enjoyed. One does not have to look for esoteric or exotic explanations for this situation. Setting aside the most obvious obstacle of language, the reasons are quite clear. There is, in the first place, the general, and often vaguely held, recognition that these poems have exerted an enormous influence on subsequent literature. This recognition frequently begins during a serious reading of Dante, who acknowledges and manifests the importance of the troubadours for him and his work in a number of ways, and concludes with a concentrated reading of the English love lyric generated and sustained by the Petrarchan tradition. Though this tradition is understood as being indebted to the poetry of the troubadours via the *dolce stil novo*, most readers and students have had to rely (and with good reason) on the authority of a small number of specialists of varying degrees of literary and critical expertise for their "background" information. Recognition also comes in the form of the quest to understand the roots and ramifications of the nature of love in the western world, an endeavor which at best adduces the poetry as evidence to an argument for a particular interpretation of the history of sexual love in our culture. In either case, or in both taken together—as they often are—it is an unfortunate situation, for which no one in particular is to blame: a high art has been reduced to a remote, if important, historical cause of cultural and literary effects that are intellectually and linguistically more accessible and of greater popular interest.

Recently the language barrier has been lessened by the publication of numerous reliable translations of the troubadours into modern English and other languages. Old Provençal, or Occitan as some prefer to call it, is not easily understood even by a person fluent in French. These translations, done mainly by scholars, have been complemented by important new critical studies by medievalists, like Frederick Goldin and L. T. Topsfield (to mention two writing in English), who have produced major accounts of the technical and thematic development of the troubadour lyric. The appearance of these translations and criticism along with better editions of many of the poets, marks a new level of interest in the poems of the troubadours as poems and in their historical and courtly contexts. Significant research and analysis is being done, as well, on the melodies that were sometimes composed for the poems or sometimes to which the poems were set. And "courtly love/ amour courtois," the great controversial aspect of the poetry, continues to provide matter for debate—over its origins, over its exact definition, over whether or not amour courtois ever existed. It is activity like this that will one day help bring about something approaching a balance between our knowledge of the poetry and the importance we have accorded it.

I do not know if there is a meaningful connection between the situation I have just described and the fact that Paul Blackburn's translations of the troubadours, which have been ready and waiting for publication since the late 1950's, are being published now, two decades later. I suspect a number of factors have caused this delay, if that is what it is. It was Ezra Pound, of course, who did more than any other twentieth-century poet to introduce the troubadours and their legacy to the English-speaking world, especially

America. Stimulated by a London literary milieu in which Provence was already something of a vogue, as Hugh Kenner has shown in *The Pound Era*, Pound not only wrote about the troubadours, as in *The Spirit of Romance* and other criticism, but he also translated some of them and adapted others, as in his *Personae;* he also worked some of their lives and lines into *The Cantos.* In short, he extended their legacy into the practice of making poetry in this century. But Pound's involvement with this poetry was limited by his interests in other matters; and, though his work with it—particularly his translations of Arnaut Daniel—pointed in the direction of the desired end of a more complete representation of troubadour poetry by a poet, he was not the man for the job. Paul Blackburn *was.* Acutely clued in to the various poetic energies that were current at mid-century, educated, able and willing to take on the serious study of Old Provençal, and biased by temperament and taste, if not by birth, towards Mediterranean and Latin culture (a serious joke he made often), Blackburn heard and understood the appeal and cue for action in Pound's initial contribution. He devoted himself to the study and translation of the troubadours as one of his central commitments to poetry. It turned out to be for life. I cannot help but believe the publication of this volume is of historic significance, as I know for sure that it was a fateful decision he made almost three decades ago to share his career with the poets in this book.

In what was probably the last resumé he prepared, Blackburn included a concise account of his training and early work on the translation project:

> I first studied *occitan ancien* (Old Provençal) with Professor Karl Bottke at the University of Wisconsin, 1949-50. I continued my reading and studies alone for a few years, and by 1953 had published a small volume of a dozen translations with the texts *en face* (*Proensa*, Divers Press, Mallorca). I believe that the independent work and subsequent publication was chiefly responsible for my Fulbright award in 1954. . . . Two years of study at [the Uni-

versity of] Toulouse saw most of the basic research on the anthology done. My studies were chiefly in occitan linguistics with Professor Jean Seguy, social anthropology of the region with Dr. René Nelli, and some Catalan literature courses. Summer 1956 to Fall 1957 were spent mostly living in Malaga and Banyalbufar, Mallorca (living is cheaper in Spain and I was living on my own savings by that time), translating, reading, re-reading, making final choices, doing constant revisions—plus my own poems.

Although the basic work had been done in this period and the resultant manuscript had been tentatively accepted for publication by a major commercial house in the spring of 1958, the book never saw the light of day. Blackburn's plans to write a long introduction to the book were interrupted by the complications and consequences of a divorce from his first wife. By the time he returned to the work two years later, he decided to undertake major revisions of the translations and to provide a section of footnotes for each poet. At the time of his death in the autumn of 1971, he had completed his revisions; the fact that some of the pages in the then final typescript contain handwritten changes indicates that he was constantly on the lookout for improvements, a normal preoccupation among translators. Since these changes were made invariably in the interests of accuracy, economy, and melody, the texts below contain these last revisions as nearly as I have been able to ascertain them. The annotation, however, proved to be a major task which went very slowly, and Blackburn was able to complete notes for only twelve of the thirty sections of the book (see note on the footnotes below). But the work of the translations was truly finished to his satisfaction.

There are, of course, some minor matters that reflect the conditions under which the work was begun and completed, matters which Blackburn would probably have taken into account had he lived to prepare his anthology for press. The most noteworthy of these are textual. First, the few poems in this volume which are now considered to be of doubtful authorship, I have allowed to stand in Blackburn's original attributions, having identified them in my notes. Second, a small number of poems in this selection received superior textual editing after Blackburn had completed his versions of them. That his translations are poetic recreations in our language, is argument enough for refraining from violating their special integrity. Besides, he always comes up with solutions that work in his poem: a close comparative reading of his translation of Marcabru's "Ges l'estornels non s'oblida" with the recently re-edited original text and translation by Goldin in *Lyrics of the Troubadours and Trouvères* will reveal the nature of some of the problems Blackburn faced and the ingenuity with which he solved them. The only matter on which I would have overruled him had I been able to, would have been to include here the version of Arnaut Daniel's "Trucs Malucs" that he mentions in his notes on that poet, but I have not succeeded in finding it (if it still exists) among any of the materials I have consulted and worked with.

At the end of an interview on translation conducted and published by *New York Quarterly* and reprinted in *The Journals* (1975), Blackburn concluded:

> I do enjoy translating, getting into other people's heads. Thass right . . .
> This is one motivation for translation. Are there others? There must be . . .

It is one of the most trenchant commentaries in English on the art of creative translation and deserves the attention of anyone interested in the subject. There are a few essential points: the translator must "let another man's life enter his own deeply enough to become some permanent part of his original author"—the getting into another person's head (and vice-versa); he should love, at least admire, what he reads in the original, recognizing their affinities; he must be guided by a realistic desire "to make an equivalent value," to settle usually for a single meaning ("Overtones are constantly being lost. Let him approach polysemia crosseyed, coin in hand.") He must understand that translation does not primarily involve the preservation of form; he must have a good sense of the audience he addresses and understand that he is doing complicated work; and finally, he must be, in Blackburn's initial definition of a translator, "A man who brings it *all* back home./In short, a madman." If this last statement seems to reduce his viewpoint to epigrammatic subjectivity, it does not conflict with the clarity of Blackburn's response to one of the central questions:

> What is the difference between free and strict, literal translation? between free translation and outright adaptation?

> Very often readability. Strict translation usually makes for stiff English, or forced and un-english rhythms. Outright adaptation is perfectly valid if it makes a good, modern poem. Occasionally, an adaptation will translate the spirit of the original to better use than any other method: at other times, it will falsify the original beyond measure. Much depends upon the translator (also upon the reader).

This late interview constitutes a poet's theory of translation that must have evolved through the decades of work on these and poems from other languages as well. But it is primarily the articulation of what were the definitive practical qualities of the experience and process that yielded the achievements of this collection, most finely realized, in my opinion, in the translations from the works of Guillem IX, Marcabru, Peire Vidal, Bertran de Born, the Monk of Montaudon, and Peire Cardenal. That he got into their heads and let them into his own is one way of saying he did not just translate them but that he gave himself, poet and man, to them. "Much depends upon the translator." Such service does not go unrewarded, and the permanent part of the returns will no doubt be enunciated in future studies of Blackburn's own poetry.

To illustrate the theory in practice, I offer a poem by Guillem IX, "Ab la dolchor del temps novel," in the original with an interlinear literal translation. A comparative reading with Blackburn's translation on pages 21-22, should give us some sense of the process that resulted in the modern English poem. Such a comparative reading should also dispel any notions that original texts (which are quite accessible these days) are aesthetically or educationally essential to this volume; for parallel appreciation of both versions can be done with confidence and edification only by those who already enjoy some proficiency in Old Provençal.

Ab la dolchor del temps novel
In the sweetness of the season new
Foillo li bosc, e li aucel
Leaf out the woods and the birds
Chanton chascus en lor lati
Sing each in its Latin/gibberish
Segon lo vers del novel chan;
According to the verses of a new song
Adonc esta ben c'om s'aisi
Then it is good that a man ease himself
D'acho don hom a plus talan.
With that gift to a man is most to his liking
  (which)

De lai don plus m'es bon e bel
From there whence most to me is good and beautiful
Non vei mesager ni sagel,
Not I see messenger nor seal(ed) (letter)
Per que mos cors non dorm ni ri,
Wherefore my heart neither sleeps nor smiles/laughs
Ni mo m'aus traire adenan,
Nor I dare to proceed forward
Tro qe sacha ben de la fi
Until I know for sure about the end/peace
S'el'es aissi com eu deman.
Whether it is such as I ask for

La nostr' amor vai enaissi
Our love goes thus
Com la branca de l'albespi
Like the branch of the hawthorn

Qu'esta sobre l'arbre tremblan,
That is on/above the tree trembling
La nuoit, a la ploja ez al gel,
The night in the rain and the frost
Tro l'endeman, que·l sols s'espan
Til the next day when the sun spreads itself
Per las fueillas verz e·l ramel.
Through the leaves green and the branches

Enquer me membra d'un mati
Still me reminds of one morning
Que nos fezem de guerra fi,
When we made of war end
E que'm donet un don tan gran,
And when me she gave a gift so great
Sa drudari' e son anel:
Her love and her ring
Enquer me lais Dieus viure tan
Yet me let God to live long enough
C'aja mas manz soz so mantel!
That I have my hands under her cloak

Qu'eu non ai soing d'estraing lati
I not (have) care for the strange gibberish/Latin
Que·m parta de mon Bon Vezi,
That me would part from my Good Neighbor
Qu'eu sai de paraulas com van
For I know about words how they go
Ab un breu sermon que s'espel,
A brief talk that spreads itself abroad
Que tal se van d'amor gaban,
Such as go around of love boasting/mocking
Nos n'avem la pessa e·l coutel.
We have the piece (of bread) and the knife

Les Chansons de Guillaume IX, ed. Alfred Jeanroy, Les classiques français du moyen âge (9), Paris, 1967, pp. 24-26.

We might note at the outset that Blackburn does not attempt to preserve the formal elements of the poem, just as he had said in the interview on translation. He never tries to "xerox" such features as line length or rhyme scheme. Yet each strophe is rendered fully, its meaning intact, as he breaks the lines according to his own voice. The addition of a word like "softest" in I.5, or the paraphrasing of II.1 as "But from where my joy springs," are characteristic of his technique, which is always faithful to what is happening and being suggested in the original. Responding to the importance to the poem of the memory that is evoked in IV, he begins the strophe with "Remembering" and emphasizes it with repetitions in the fifth and last lines. The addition of "as sign" as the entire preceding line, besides having an important rhythmic function, explains the significance of the Lady's gesture of giving her ring. In the literature of courtly love such a gift betokened her willingness to grant her love —in word and eventually in deed. Thus, the translator makes literal in his version what was metaphorical in the original in order to insure its meaning and to prepare for the poem's moment of greatest intensity and sensuality: "I pray to God I live to put my hands/ under her cloak, remembering that."

The rhyme scheme of the original employs three rhymes which are distributed in two different orders but in a single pattern throughout: AABCBC (first two strophes) BBCACA (last three strophes). The shift in order in III attends the poem's turning from the description of spring (a standard opening), its effect on the lovers and his feeling of insecurity, to a description of the nature of their love in the past and his confident hopes for the future. The shift constitutes a variation on what was probably the most common and one of the least difficult of troubadour rhyme schemes (which could be quite intricate), *coblas unisonans*, the same rhyme scheme with the same end rhymes throughout. It could be argued that this variation suggests—along with other evidence—that Guillem, the earliest troubadour with extant work, was working within a tradition that was already well-developed. Whatever its literary, rhetorical, semantic, or musical implications, the rhyme scheme of the original poem cannot transcend the historical contingencies of its performance(s) in Old Provençal. Blackburn knew not only this

xxi

but also the audience for whom he was remaking the poem. He gives up what can never be reclaimed anyway; but then he preserves meaning through an equivalence that is shaped by his sense of himself as a poet and by his understanding of the needs of his readers and listeners.

In the final strophe of "Ab la dolchor," see how he uses apposition and description to emphasize the role of the bitter talkers, the divisive gossips of the courtly lyric; yet he incorporates a literal translation of the essential "d'amor gaban." These are the mocking, two-faced enemies of love and lovers whom Chaucer calls "losengeours." Blackburn neutralizes them with the phrase "No matter," evoking the Chaucerian "No fors," which asserts the supremacy of all fine lovers over their jealous detractors. This negation of the enemy is brilliantly counterbalanced by the positive note in his rendering of "Nos n'avem," the emphatic double pronoun in the last line:

"We are the ones, we have
    some bread, a knife."

It should be evident by now that the art of translation as practiced by a poet like Blackburn is also an act of interpretation. "Much depends upon the translator." That is why his scholarly credentials are important, too, for each of his versions is the result of a complex blending of creativity and *scientia*. It is in this context that his work must be accepted and evaluated. In this context we can accept his occasionally resorting to an anachronism (see his note on Peire d'Alvernhe, page 284, and mine on Marcabru, page 279); we can applaud his tendency to concretize and illustrate what his Provençal original presented generally and as common knowledge. This kind of interpolation is well exemplified by the opening of Peire Vidal's "Ab l'alen tir vas me l'aire" (page 108). (The poem celebrates the origins and self-consciousness of the poet, praises Provence as a country and as the home of his lady, who in turn is praised as the source of everything excellent he has and is.) Blackburn introduces into the poem's first strophe those "dockside taverns" where the poem's narrator hears "travelers' gossip told" in order to satisfy the greater craving of the contemporary reader than of his medieval counterpart for an immediate and concrete setting and starting point. But most of all, the first line of this poem reveals the poet who is always at work in these versions. The first two lines of Vidal's poem, "Ab l'alen tir vas me l'aire/qu'eu sen venir de Proensa (With my breath I draw towards me the air/that I feel coming from Provence)," are combined into one:

I suck deep in air come from Provence to here.

As we read the line we become conscious of our own breathing; the sequence of the words and the cadence of their syllables makes us draw in the air of our own present reading of—and thus physically implicates us in—the praise of both poets for the homeland of *trobar*.

A NOTE ON THE FOOTNOTES

The notes Blackburn prepared for twelve of the poets in this book are distinctive for their readability, scholarly soundness, and critical acumen: in his note on Guillem IX's "Farai un vers de dreyt nien," for example, he nicely anticipates L. T. Topsfield on the parodic elements in Guillem's poems. In the few instances that I have provided additional information in these notes, I have identified them as mine in the following way: [E:]. In the notes I have provided for the rest of the poets, I have limited myself to annotating only those details that are essential for basic comprehension of the sense of the texts.

All special terms that pertain to the study of troubadour poetry are defined in the notes. The *vidas* and *razos* that precede the poetry selections were composed in the thirteenth and fourteenth centuries 8long after the poets' lifetimes. While they are bound to contain some historical truth, they also contain a good deal of invention. Very often the main source of their information is merely the poetry of the very subjects they introduce and explain. It is generally agreed that the *razos* (literally, reasons) often provided a background, whether historically accurate or purely legendary, for the performance of the songs. Questions of historical reliability aside, many of them deserve to be regarded as a kind of literary criticism. It is typical of the translator's gracious character that he composed a *vida* for the troubadour Giraut Riquier, the old one having been lost or, more likely, never written.

From the selection by Bernart Arnaut de Moncuc (pp. 234 ff.) to the end, a number of the poems deal with aspects of the Albigensian Crusade and its aftermath.

GUILLEM IX, DUKE OF AQUITAINE

(1071—1127)

VIDA

The count of Poitou was certainly one of the greatest knights in the world, and was very unfaithful toward women. A good man with weapons and open-handed at courting, he sang well also and knew trobar. And he went for a long time through the world deceiving women.

He had a son who married the duchess of Normandy, by whom he had a daughter who married King Henry of England. She was mother of the young king, of Lord Richard, and of Count Geoffrey of Brittany.

Companho, faray un vers . . . covinen

I'm going to make a vers boys, . . . good enough?
But I witless, and it most mad and all
mixed up, mesclatz, jumbled from youth and love and joy—

And if the vulgar do not listen to them?
Learn 'em by heart? He takes a hard
parting from men's love who composes to his own liking.

I have two horses for my saddle, sleek,
game: but husband both for battle? I've
not the skill, for neither will allow the other.

But if I could fasten them both to serve my rein
I would not change cavalage with any other,
for then I'd be better mounted than any man living.

The first is of mountain-stock, the swifter running,
her walk sure-footed, well-composed, but is wild
shy, fierce, so savage she forbids currying. The other

was nourished up and bred past Cofolens, and
you've never seen one more beautiful, take my word.
I won't trade that one off, not for gold or silver.

I gave her to her lord a grazing colt, yet
by the saints, I've trained her so that she
at my sign would rive her bridle asunder, to come to me.

Gentlemen, in this difficulty, counsel me!
Never was I more harassed in a choice.
Agnes or Arsen! Madness or death will take me first.

At Gimel I have a castle under domain.
at Nieul I've pride before men, for both
these nonpareils are sworn to me, and pledged by oath.

2

Compaigno, non puosc mudar qu'eo no·m effrei

I've heard the talk
I now have proof before me, and
friends
      I am all precaution;
for a certain lady makes complaint to me
          of her custodians.

She says she will not be tethered by right or law,
that they keep her corked up in captivity,
      close to the three of them;
and if one gives slack rein a little, the others
        will tighten the cinches.

And that there is no point of agreement among them:
      one, a charming companion,
gives voice like a push-cart vendor.
Set together they conduct a fracas louder than
        all the king's helots.

      And I tell you jailkeepers,
        I warn you—
and it would be very stupid to disbelieve me—
that you will be hard put to it to find a sentry who
will not sleep for a crucial
        half-hour
           now and again.

For I know of no woman, trustworthy or not,
who does not want her own way in her affairs,
        to give or refuse,
and if she is forced, will turn to any contrivance.

If you don't stock select groceries for her larder, she
          will eat what's at hand.

If she cannot have the war-horse, then
                she'll buy the trotter. And

there is no one of you can dissuade me from her.
       Wine, say, is prohibited one
              for reasons of health.
                     Die of thirst then? No,
I think, then, one would drink water.

Anyone will drink water rather than die of thirst.

Companho, tant ai agutz d'avols conres

So much bad food and worse liquor, friends,
can't hardly get this song out, and that
      doesn't bother me, hear?
              In fact,
                      it's better
not everyone know the depth of my affairs.

Let me tell you clear
my intention in this is: not
to be pleased with my own caution, nor
in mill-races without fish, nor the gabble
of evil-minded men, the like of which,
                    YOU KNOW
I would not have said about them . . .

Lord,
God,
king and governor of the world, who
ever set guard over a cunt when he had not first used it?
      And he whose case
                  never had need of a watchman,
      without exception
                  treats his lady the worst.

But let me tell you about cunt:
                  it's his religion,
that man who spreads no gossip nor listens to worse.
But that other thing dwarfs, finally, what steals from it,
and cunt at this point rises to it, prospers from it,
                  generally, flourishes thereby.

And those who choose not to believe my reproaches
will whinny and poke around bushes in perpetual tangle.
But if a man chop down a tree, does it not follow
that two or three will spring up to replace it?

And when the timber is cut off, it grows up again more thickly,
and the gentlemen loses neither his computation nor his mind.
Quite the reverse. A man can regret the damage (once he has done
      it).

It is wrong (to do) damage without (having regretted it).

Farai un vers de dreyt nien

I shall make a vers about
    nothing,
downright nothing, not
about myself or youth or love
    or anyone.
    I wrote it horseback dead asleep
while riding in the sun.

I was born—don't know the hour,
not blood nor choler has the power.
My humour's neither sweet nor sour;
    not worth a drop
since the night they sorcered me
    on a mountaintop.

Don't know if I'm awake or sleep
if no one comes to fill me in.
My heart is nearly cleft with pain
    (it rather it were partial).
I wouldn't give you a mouse for it
    by old Saint Martial.

I guess I'm sick enough to die,
know only what they tell me. I'll
ask the doc for what I want, I
    don't know what it can be.
I'll recommend his doctoring if
    ever he can heal me, but
if I sicken and get worse, well
    maybe not, maybe not.

I have a friend, I don't know who
for I have never seen her. So
she treats me neither well nor ill,
    I do not say I blame her.

But this argument is also nil, it
    is not worth a curse
since I've never had a Norman or
    a Frenchman in the house.

Never saw her and I love her
very much. It doesn't matter if
she treats me straight or not, for I
    do very well without her,
and besides, I know another who is
    prettier and such.
Why, she is not worth a rooster, and
    this other one is rich!

Well. I've made the vers already, though
    I do not know of whom. And I shall
    send it to a friend of mine who's
        sitting in a room.
He will hand it to another near Anjou,
    a gravel pit, who may
send me back from out his box, someday,
        the key to it.
    Box or vers, the key to it.

Farai un vers pos mi sonelh

I'll make a vers while I'm asleep here
walking and loafing in the sun.
  Some women play a lot of nasty games,
   I could name names,
women who disdain to take a knight as lover.

They commit a heavy mortal sin
refusing a loyal nobleman;
  and if they love a monk or clerk
   then they are wrong.
By rights, one might then use a torch
   to make them burn.

   Beyond Limousin, in the Auvergne,
   going along there under my cloak
   alone, I met the wives of en Gari
    and en Bernart;
   they greeted me simply in the name
    of St. Leonart.

   And one said to me in her dialect:
    "God save you, sir pilgrim.
   You seem of decent family
    in my opinion.
   We see traveling through the world
    too many madmen."

Now hear what I said to them:
I answered neither pack nor point
nor mentioned either staff nor tool,
but only said, "Tarra babart
  marta babelio riben
   saramahart."

Agnes said to Ermessaine: "We've
found what we were looking for.
God's love, sister, let's take him in,
he's as dumb as our bedroom door.
No one will ever know the tricks
    we used him for."

    One of them took me beneath her cape,
    brought me into their room by the fireplace.
    You know, that made me feel very nice?
        and the fire was good.
    And I warmed myself at the huge coals
        and burning wood.

    They had me eat—a few capons, and
    understand, there were more than two!
    And neither cook nor scullery boys
    but the three of us for supper.
    And the bread was white and the wine was good
        and lots of pepper.

"Sister, this fellow here is clever
and's holding his tongue because of us.
Let's bring in our great red cat
who'll make him babble soon enough
    if he lies in this matter."

Agnes went for the ugly beast. His
whiskers were long and his claws immense.
I saw him among us and was in terror.
I nearly forgot that I was fearless
    and full of valor.

    When we had drunk and eaten well,
    I undressed myself, at their request.
    She held behind my back, that cat—
        vicious and cruel—

and dragged him from my second rib
    down to my heel.

She seized the cat then by the tail,
    swung him and clawed me.
They gave me more than a hundred rips that day,
but I would scarcely have budged yet
    if they had killed me.

"Sister," said Agnes to Ermessaine,
"he's real dumb, that much is plain.
Draw him a bath, and after that
    we'll have some lovin'."
Eight days and more they kept me there
    in that damned oven!

Now hear how many times I fucked them:
a hundred-and-eighty and eight times more,
until I nearly broke my strap
    and the baggage with it.
And I can't tell you how much it stung
    he took so much of it.

I can hardly tell you about the pain,
    he stood so much of it.

tornada

At daybreak, Ned, roll off the couch.
You'll carry this song in your pouch
straight to the wives of en Gari
    and en Bernat,
and tell them, see, for love of me
    that they KILL THAT CAT!

Ben vuelh que sapchon li pluzor

        I would like it if people knew this song,
        a lot of them, if it prove to be okay
        when I bring it in from my atelier, all
        fine and shining:
        for I surpass the flower of this business,
        it's the truth, and I'll
        produce the vers as witness
        when I've bound it in rhyme.

Good sense? I know, and foolishness,
and disgrace *and* domain: I've
known panic and all of valor. But
give me a tenso on love, I'm no such fool
that I cannot choose the better side
against the ill.

I know who they are who use a spate
of fine words to me,
who, when they turn their backs, make signs
for my ill-luck: likewise
I differentiate who it is mocks me in secret,
and who takes honest pleasure in my company.
So as a matter of course I ought to choose
whether I work for their end, or their repose.

        O, bless them who brought me up and fit me
        for such fine business!
        for never have I had bad success with any.
        I know how to play on top of pillows at
        any throw, and I
        have it on the best assurances
        that none of my neighbors
        has anywhere near my talent.

I praise St. Julian and God, I've
learned this gentle sport so well
(and I have a good hand for it, I tell
you), that I'm an expert twice.
Whoever asks my counsel will not be refused
or leave without carrying off *some* advice.

For I have earned the name of "Old Infallible":
never a mistress who had me one night
didn't want me again in the morning.
I've been so well taught in this business
(I'm bragging here)
that thanks to that I can earn my bread
at any market.

Don't think I'm joking now, but I
was not put out the other day, laying
large stakes at hazard.
They did too well giving me the first play,
I went down on the table.
My turn to watch—I saw no one beat my score,
in fact, all of 'em crapped out.

But then she reproached me:
"Sir
your dice were too light
and I bid you at doubles."
"I wouldn't turn that down," said I
"if they gave me Montpellier."
I palmed the dice
and lifted her gaming table a bit
with both my arms.

And when I had lifted the table, I
made my throw with the dice:
two of them straddled the line, and the third
went plumb down the center.

And I made the stroke into the table strong
and cried,
  "GAME!"

Pus vezem de novelh florir

WHEN WE SEE AGAIN the spring blossoming of the world,
    orchards and meadows growing green one more time,
brooks and springs clear-running, fresh-running winds,
then that every living man should take full measure
    of what gives him pleasure.

I ought to say nothing but good of Love,
but now? when I have neither gift nor salary
        of him? All
right,
I clip a bit more than I agree to. But
        how easily
        and what great joy
he gives to those who support his arrangements.

        Always, I take it,
            never can I take
            pleasure of those I love;
yet neither do I miss by slow application.
Yet, when to my knowledge you make it
with several other men in a row, my
            heart says to me:
            "It is nothing."

Through such reasonings
I have less of that fine
knowledge than the others,
and I want whatever it is I cannot have.
But if I can last out the proverb that says so, then most certainly,
        "To good heart shall be added good courage, in
        him who is sufficiently patient."
                (which is ghastly).

Indeed,
there will be no man entirely faithful toward Love
if he have not surrendered his balls,
and is not equally pleasant to strangers
    and neighbors of her
    whom he would love.
As for those who live under the same roof with her,
        he must be
        minutely
            attentive to the movements,
            even the vagaries of
                their bowels.
                Yet

he ought to wear openly his devotion to the people
of her whom he wishes to love.
            And it helps
            if he know how
            to make his conduct attractive;
        and if in court
        he manage to not
    make speeches like a farmer .

Concerning this vers, I tell you, it's
        worth the most to him who best
        understands and rejoices in it.
All the words are equally ordered to the same measure, and
the tune, for I praise it myself, is a fine, brave tune .

    At Narbonne (but I do not go there) my vers
        should be openly put to him,
    and I want this praise to act as my surety.

    My old Bagpipe, though I do not go there,
    my vers should be publicly sung to him,
    and this praise serve as my guarantor.

Farai chansoneta nueva

I shall make a new song now
before it blows or rains or snows,
for my lady makes a test case: how
and to what degree my fondness goes.
And no quarrel she advances against me
will get me
loose of her bond.

Rather,
I deliver myself to her, will give her
ground-rent,
if she will write me into her charter.
I'm not just liquored up, I
love this woman. Without
her, life moves toward death,
the season is bad

but,
her whiteness is
more than ivory's whiteness.
Sun is pale where this whiteness glows.
If no hope comes to me shortly, some
sign, some proof of her love,
I shall die, by the head of Saint Gregory,
unless I have of her close kiss in chamber
or under the bough.

What gain will you have of it, lady, if
your love keeps me off?
Do you like the idea of a nunnery?
And you know, my love is so great
I fear an attack of the dolors
if you do not set right those wrongs
of which I complain to you.

What good will you have of it, seriously,
if I shut myself up? And I will
if you do not keep me by you. And to think,
all the world's joys are ours, lady,
if both of us love.

Down there to my friend Daurostre, I say
and command that he sing it, not yell it.

> For her I shiver and tremble, for
> the fine love that I have for her.
> Another like her
>   has never been born
>   from the great line of Adam.

Mout jauzens me prenc en amar

LUCKILY, I take great joy of love,
wanting only to relax and enjoy it.
And wanting now
to return to such joy, I
should go to the best if I can.
And beyond all expectation, I
have credit from the fairest a
man could see or hear of.

As you know,
I do not boast or credit myself,
in the hour of composition, with
any extravagant praise.
But, if any joy could flower, this
one should
bear grain beyond all others
and gleam beyond all others,
like a dark day
broken into by sun.

No man can fashion that body in his mind,
by no turn of desire raise it by
hard thought or dream.
Such joys as I am thinking of
will find their equal nowhere.
I could not praise her properly
in a year of trying.

All joys give ground before her,
all arrogance is obedient by
reason of her soft mien,
by reason of her soft glance.
He who has joy of her will last
a hundred years at least.

There shines from her an exaltation and
the sick are made well.
Her anger would kill a paragon of health.
The wisest man goes mad, the Don Juan
moults his beauty—the peasant
feels himself ennobled, the courtier
turns to a dolt.

Since man can find no better one,
neither eye see or mouth make known,
I want
to keep her close
for my own use,
to refresh the heart within, reno-
              vate the flesh,
        then it will never grow gaunt.

If my lady will give her love
I am thankful and ready to take it,
conceal it and never boast of it,
        ready to flatter, ready to
        say and make pleasure for her and
              never count the cost,
              to prize her worth,
              promote her praises everywhere...

        I do not dare
        send the thing by another,
        I have such fear she will flare up,
        nor go myself.
        I'm so afraid of failing
I dare not assemble in strength my love's evidences;
for she knows it is through her alone
I have any healing.

Ab la dolchor del temps novel

In the new season
when the woods burgeon
and birds
sing out the first stave of new song,
time then that a man take the softest joy of her
who is most to his liking.

But from where my joy springs
no message comes:
the heart will not sleep or laugh, nor dare I go out
till I know the truth, if she will have me or not.

Our love is like top
branches that creak
on the hawthorn at night,
stiff from ice
or shaking from rain. And tomorrow
the sun
spreads its living warmth through the branches and through
the green leaves on the tree.

Remembering
the softness of that morning we put away anger,
when she gave me her love, her ring
as sign,
remembering the softness,
I pray to God I live to put my hands
under her cloak, remembering that.

And I
care not for the talk
that aims to part
my lady from me;
for I know how talk runs rife and gossip spreads
from empty rancid mouths that, soured

make mock of love.
No matter. We are the ones, we have
some bread, a knife.

Pos de chantar m' es pres talentz

Song seizes me, but my own vers gives me dolor,
and in Poitou or Limousin I'll never again be lover.

To exile now, fearful in mid of danger,
and leave my son to fight those who will give him hurt.

I lose both heart and possession quitting Poitou;
I leave Folque d'Anjou to guard the land and his cousin.

If Folque cannot hold it, he who grants me seisin
will have Angevins and Gascons on his neck.

They will see him young and feeble when I have gone
they will bring him down if his prowess be not double.

Mercy I ask of friends wherever I have wronged:
I pray to Christ in Occitan, also in Latin.

I rode in prowess and joy, leave both behind now
going hellbent to where all sinners end up.

Gaily I lived. Now God no longer cares for it:
being half-dead, even I no longer desire it.

All ceremony quit, all loving habit:
if God love me, whatever comes, I welcome it.

Friends, at my demise come do me honor:
since I've taken my pleasure all over the neighborhood too.

All gracious show I leave, joys of love and table,
two kinds of grey fur, also sable.

CERCAMON

(c. 1137—1152)

VIDA

Cercamon was a joglar* from Gascoigne, and made vers and pastorelas after the ancient usage, and visited the whole world, wherever he could get to. And for that reason he was called Cercamons.

*The joglar, or (Fr.) jongleur, was the paid musician and singer. Each had his own repertory from the songs of any number of trobadors (finders). Some troubadours, de Born or Peire Cardenal for example, had their own personal joglars who sang exclusively, or chiefly, the songs of their masters. It is difficult, mostly impossible, to know whether this was due to the individual troubadour's high position, or an ingrained sense of retirement, or an unpleasant voice, or a lack of skill with the instruments. Cercamon was a troubadour in his own right, but the biographer's designation indicates how he had to earn his living.

CERCAMON

Car vei finir a tot dia

—Seeing love end
seeing each day
merriment & sport
cease,
and the clergy no help in the matter,
I cannot deny myself that cold comfort
the swan takes when he knows his death,
when he cries out against it, when
he protests, forcing out his song
                there
                finding there is no comfort
                more, anywhere in it.

—God help me, Maistre, a fit speech, well spoken.
                But be a little above it :
don't concern yourself that the clerks are paltry
                in their dispensations.
We have a good time coming I think, and you
will have such patronage as will get you a palfrey
                or even better, an income,
                for the Count of Poitou is coming!

—Guilhalmi, what you tell me is not
worth two broken rings from a coat of mail :
                I prefer one quail
                stick to my ribs
                than a henhouse
to which someone else holds the key
                & to wait on his favor.
Who waits for another's kindness, does
more yawning than anything else.

—Still, you may have a great success, Maistre,
                if you are patient.

—Just as you say, Guilhalmi, but I don't
                believe empty mouthings.
—Maistre, you grant me no credence?
Great gain will come to you from France if
                you're willing to wait for it.
—Guilhalmi, such hope as you offer me, God
                gave you. Keep it.

—Maistre, you haven't got the courage of
                a child, of a scatterbrain.
—With good money on the table, Guilhalmi, I'd
                believe you with pleasure.
—Maistre, these men of rank
have many good chargers to carry even the
                least of their companions.
—Guilhalmi, strong and savage (is
                my hand on a rein).

—Maistre, through the bushes, new
                rooftops come into sight.
—Guilhalmi, you reckon as slight the shelter
                I have at the castle.
—Maistre, the new count we shall
have after Pentecost will pay you
                exceptionally well . . .
                —Guilhalmi, hell!
anyone who listens to you is an outright
                idiot, you're
so generous with someone else's cash.

Ab lo temps qe fai refrescar

WITH the fine spring weather
that makes the world seem young again,
when the meadows come green again
I want to begin
with a new song
on a love that's my cark and desire,
but is so far I cannot hit her mark
or my words fire her.

Nothing can comfort me ever, I'm
better off dead when foul mouths
have separated me from her, God-
       damn them! O,
I would have wanted her so much! And now
I grouch and shout, or weep, or sing
       or walk about
like any hare-brained golden thing.

You hear me sing of her and I
have no skill to tell you her loveliness.
Her glance kills, the beauty of its directness does, her
color's fresh, skin white, white without blemish, no
       she wears no makeup.
And they can say no hard word of her, so
fine, clear as an emerald, is her excellence.

       Above all else, the prize is that her word
       is true beyond doubting. With
       all her sophistication and fine speech, she
       has never wanted to deceive her lover, ever,
       and I was out of my head the day I
       trusted something I'd heard said,
          believed that she was angry.

I can make no move of censure against her, for still
she can give me joy, or take, as she will,
     and has the power to
give a thing would make me rich.
But I can't go on, losing food and sleep like this
     for so long,
          because I can no longer
          live near her . . .

When he starts out, Love is so soft,
but is so bitter when he leaves.
One day he makes you rejoice and dance,
     the next you cry out!
I know how his operations move,
for, the more I thought to serve
Love, the more he changed countenance.

          Messenger, go—God keep you fit,
          may you know to be agile before her,
          convincing when you deliver the song:
          for I feel I cannot live here long
               nor there heal,
          if I can't have her next to me kissed,
               undressed
          in curtained chamber.

CERCAMON

Per fin' amor m'esjauzira

True love
warms my heart,
no matter if he run hot or cold.
My thoughts attract on her always,
but can't know yet
if I can finish the job, stay
firm with joy, that is
if she wants to keep me hers
which my heart most desires.

I quit all lords and all ladies
if she wants me to serve her in it:
and who speaks to me of separation
will have me die tonight. I
place my hope in no other one,
sunup, sunset, night or day,
my heart dreams no other happiness.

I'd hardly have spoken out so soon
if I'd known how hard she softened. No
thing but does not humble itself toward Love—
        her? she is fierce toward him!
But a lady can have no valor, not
by riches and not by power, if
the joy of Love blow not within her.

I'd not leave her feet, if it pleasure her
if she consent to it.
If she wanted to she could enrich me, saying
she were my woman.
All the rest whatever, at her pleasure,
were it truth or lies, no matter,
        that word
would be all the wealth I'd need.

I've sat between joy and pain since
goodbyes were said, for I've not seen
her since that day. She said if I loved her
she would love me. Beyond that, I
know nothing of her intent.
But she ought to know well enough that I
will die if she keeps me in torment.

The fairest woman ever used a mirror never
saw anything soft and white as ermine,
    as she is,
fresher than lily or rose—any flower!
And nothing makes me despair more. God!
    may I enjoy the hour
when I can make love-play beside her!
No. I, no. She does not turn toward me.

My lady would fill to overflow
all my desires, if she but now
would grant—if only one—to
ease me, just one kiss.
    How I'd fight then!
war against any neighbor, give largely,
make myself feared and know, hurl
enemies down, keep my possessions, my
goods, my own.
And may my lady know that, for my part,
no man of my rank could serve her
with better heart.
    And if she pleasure me next her,
    if she let me lie next to her level,
    sure I would not die of this evil.

MARCABRU

(c. 1130—1148)

VIDAS

I.

Marcabru was left outside a rich man's door, and no one ever knew who he was or where he was from. And Sir Aldric d'Anvillars had him brought up. Afterwards, he spent a good deal of time with a troubadour called Cercamon who started him composing. At that time he was known as Panperdut, but afterward had the name Marcabru.

In those days no one called them *cansos*, but everything that was sung was called *vers*.

He was much renowned and listened to throughout the world, and feared for his language, for he made many malicious songs. In the end, some castellans of Guyenne murdered him, because he had said very evil things about them.

II.

Marcabru was from Gascoigne, son of a poor woman who was called Marcabruna, so that he says in his songs:

> Marcabrun, son of lady Brun,
> was begot in such a moon that
> he knew Love's decay, how it
> crumbles, falls in ruins. Listen!
> for never he loved anyone
> or had the love of woman.

He was a troubadour of the first rank, as man remembers. He made some vicious *sirventes*, and spoke badly of women and of love.

Aujatz de chan com enans' e meillura

Now hear this!
HEAR THIS!
how our song
betters itself,
always at thrust
how, following his distinct grasp, Marcabru
knows how to weave
subject and theme,
to so accord the vers that no man can
pluck from the line
a word.

Lord, how they enjoy it!
'I had not thought there were so many'
whose sole delight is in wickedness, that
grows and grows worse in its excess.
But what summons me to be an enemy is
that this bitch *likes* to hear me roar and cry.

O, the vilest are destined for rewards
and the best stand gaping
mouths wide before an empty simulacrum.
The narrative alone makes me gloomy,
and the rich conduct their business on their heads.

No more hope in Youth, he
's already turned jay-dee, and
against Death there's neither roof
nor help
These creeps have already thrown Youth
off the plot
and driven him from the roads. His mother's fault.

That man who, for profit, discounts shame and measure,
who ignores

honor and valor when he acts,
seems to me he's colleague to the hedgehog,
confrère of the mongrel and the thief.

Prowess breaks and Baseness mans the walls,
will not let Joy come within the enclosure.
Who sees any reason or right maintained, when
a drunken riffraff rogue is emperor for gain?

Count of Poitou, your valor has grown firmer,
and that of Amfos of Toulouse as well,
                however little,
but now Provence, Avignon, Beaucaire are held better
than the Toulousain alone was by his father.

          If the count of Toulouse
          contents himself with
          making me welcome,
and otherwise seems skimpy and close-fisted,
I know another Amfos over near León,
frank, reasonable, courteous and open-handed,
          a generous man.

May holy writ keep from evil all who show
themselves unaffected and nakedly: may
          Amfos who is, and was, king
          and rescuer of kings,
show me a welcome light to his waiting hall.

L'autrier jost' un sebissa

Under a hedge the other day
I noticed a low-born shepherdess,
full of wit and merriment
and dressed like a peasant's daughter:
her shift was drill, her socks were wool,
clogs and a fur-lined jacket on her.

I went to her across the field:
—O baby, what a pretty piece...
You must be frozen, the winds increase,
—Sir, said the girl to me,
thanks to my nurse and God, I care
little that wind ruffle my hair,
I'm happy and sound.

—Look, honey, I said, after all,
I turned in here and out of my way
just to keep you company.
Such a peasant girl ought not
without a proper fellow
pasture so many beasts alone
in such wild country.

—Sire, she said, be what I may,
the difference between sense and tom-
foolery I know. Your company,
     said the maid to me,
should be offered to someone worthy
of it. Though, whoever got it
wouldn't have much to brag of.

—Demoiselle of noble line, he
must have been a knight, your father,
he who got you in your mother,
and she herself a noble peasant.

The more I look the better I like,
it'd be a pleasure to make you happy
if only you'd act a bit human.

—Noble sir, my family line
I see returning time and time
again to pitchfork and plow,
    said the girl to me.
And I know of some playing at knight
that ought to be using the same set
    six days of the week.

—Girl, I said, a gentle fairy
gave you a beauty at your birth
fine and shining as an emerald
    over any other maid.
And you'd be twice as lovely if,
just once, you'd close with me a bit,
I above and you beneath.

—You have so flattered me, my lord,
I'm completely floored with praise.
And since you've raised my worth so high,
    said the maid to me,
I shall give you as reward in
parting: your mouth's open, son,
and the waste of an afternoon.

—Little one, the heart that's wild
and shy, man tames by use. I can
tell from such small-talk that one
might have a fine relationship with
    such a girl as you . . .
a rich and heartfelt friendship,
    if both were true.

—Any man who's hard up, sir, will
promise the moon and swear to gord . . .
and that's how you pay your homage, sir,
    said the girl to me.
And for such a cheap entrance-fee
you expect I'll leave virginity
    to earn the name of whore?

—Girl, take my word,
every creature reverts to nature.
Let's just lie down together, love,
alongside the pasture where there's cover,
for then you will feel free to do
    the softest things.

—Yes sir, but to reason a bit:
fools seek their own folly by nature,
nobles, some noble undertaking.
It's peasants seek a peasant girl.
If measure's not kept then wisdom's lacking,
    at least the old folks say so.

—About faces, wench, I'm not demanding
but I've never seen one looked more a tart,
    and as for hearts . . .
never one more inhuman.

—Sir, the owl is your bird of omen.
There's always some who'll stand open-
    mouthed before the simple show,
while there's others'll wait until the
    lunch basket comes around.

A l'alena del vent doussa

God sends us from I don't know where
a gentle mawkish wind. One breath
                    and surfeited with joy,
                    I have some heart against
the ruddy blandness of the season when
these fields are turned crisp yellow and vermillion.

                    I like it now,
                    the mountains in shadow
and birds under the weeds mix
cries in with their songs, and
each, with whatever voice he has, is
                    festive in the ditch
                    with his lady.

Which locus smelleth. Ah. It is the stench
from where they caught their crotch-hair in the bushes
            who are so in demand,
the spoil-breads, the cut-worms in the cut, i.e., they
            guard the ladies
whom no stranger, save the master, is to touch.

Now, if all the husbands give their wives a hug
            and go off reassured, and all
            the guardians are overjoyed,
the liturgy and response are hardly equal.
For they walk boldly in the light, who
            at night, go without a lamp,
and touch the same jug for just a sample.

                    These 'honorable' guards
                    keep their distance from him
with their gross, fleshly lusts and shifty plans.
But Marcabru knows what the hell

is going on and says:
the jealous fools themselves
making cattle-contract with these crawlers
put our wives into the game as well.

Harshly, I dream of giving gift
to extricate myself from this dirty business,
no, not gift. Better call it pay. This egg.
By nature they've all the tendencies of dogs;
like any mangy mutt or peevish hound, instead
of waiting for a portion,
they hover over the pot and blow at the flame.

There is no key nor means to keep them
from having at what is best hidden.
First fruit and second fruit.
And they see to it their viciousness is well concealed,
and see we're given 'NO' instead of 'Enter'.

The jealous husband, when, in his fine
madness, swells
farts and is emptied
recast immediately into his usual
font of stupidity,
he should know he's managing a whore:
except then, he'd always have the poor
but true excuse
that he'd always been inefficient.

Contra l'ivern que s'enansa

Against winter which advances
and the hard thoughts which assail me,
I find it's good the song lances
that I let it sail
                    out
before another trouble finds me.
That one project lets me down
doesn't mean I need another one
                    to compensate me . . .

But, if I sit here in this state
of mind and find I'm hoisted up
to ambiguity's rack,
by this girl who tortures me, who
keeps me in balance,
forward . . . . back, but toward
her with just the final weight,
it is that with a soft savour
she primes her hook,
using soft words for bait.

            My desire
        and her semblance
        are and are not
        on the same level
in this dance,
for it's desire that gives the semblance birth,
although with words she squirm and modify it.
        Say one's desire catches the gull,
            oneself,
                and that the birdlime's weak,
                her word
smears the poor bird once more to keep him down.

Bitterness—
you'll find no lack of it in this clown,
the consequences of love's dull tricks.
But I'd love even the bitterness
if she loved me in love, giving me
        even the feeble recompense
          that I deserve.

I hope she still wants to see me.
I have such expectation to serve
I even expect the association to
have, in fact, a long duration:
for, though in the midst of this mad business
        I never speak a word of madness.

But he who lays his trust in love, I assure you,
will be left yawning in front of her door
many a night,
will stand around wasting his time, for
this love of mine
loves to complicate things—
it'd take an engineer to ravel them out.

It's with unworthy desire, estrangement, knockdown & drag-out
that Love repays lovers who are over-desirous. Me,
I show only about-faces to him,
defend myself
unpredictably.
If I have to take arrogance from a woman
I pay her out with her own medicine.

The merit of her I sing is sovereign without contest.
And her effectiveness is sovereign
even if one contest it.
And if it isn't she who awakes me
don't imagine anyone else will.

He knows not from whence it moves
who made the vers and dances it.

Marcabru has made the dance
but does not know who started it.

Puois la fuoilla revirola

When the leaf spins
its staying power
                    gone,
twists off,
        falls
                    spinning
down through the branches
from top limbs from
which the wind has
                    torn it, I
watch.
It is a sign.
                    The icy storm that's brewing's better
                    than grumbling and meandering summer
                    congesting us with hates and whoring.

        Peace.
                    Nightingale and magpie turn
                        their songs to silence.
        The same with oriole and jay; winter
                        has its will.
For a season anyway
into the gutter goes the pride
of the blackguarding, bobtailed riff-raff, who
in summer are not afraid to make
                    a show of teeth.

Toads who toady up and snakes that sneak
are to be expected and should frighten no one;
horse flies, blow flies,
                    they, we know
                    live on carrion.
        All of them now cold, toads,
snakes, flies, scarabs, hornets, all,
I cannot hear their buss nor, happily,

smell their stink.
We drink old winter who's delivered us,
    our smiles and wine.

But take that fellow there, say, his
beak filed with an adze,
he doesn't lose his place in the foyer,
but he carries a pic and a little mace
which two together can cause some hurt.
And from being too much in bed with his mistress
    his cock hurts.
It's more than his master can say.

He takes an armful of honey morning and night,
can even get it between the bands of a corset.
He knows how to wiggle his ass. The vavassor,
he does his day's work at night,
    it gets him a son.
So instead of a vassal's vassal, he becomes
    the lord's lord.

As that little stork slumps, rises and sinks again,
mounting and bending down, the world's in the vortex,
whirling. I'm indifferent, me.
There are eyes that will not see
that will not recognize spoiled goods, even
now when the service of Love is given
    over to harlotry.

                    Marcabru?
you'll hardly find him
sniffing in a corner, he knows the score.
His lady's of the good school where
                    Joy is master.
And when the license is given outright
he always extends himself a mite
    more than he has to.

I pray to God he do not take
Guissart to his celestial kingdom, for
the battle axe he uses here works
      better
in this best of all sensual worlds,
    and he has left an inheritor.
And I'll never again have faith in a son
    if this one
    doesn't resemble his father.

But to return to these birds,
despaired of reaching the clouds, and being
    by nature fools, they bow
for all (and more than) they're worth.
      And whether or not it's said amiss,
      barons who sell out for cash
      have hearts below their umbilicus.

He has his heart below his unwashed navel,
    that noble baron
    who dirties himself for cash.

Estornel, cueill ta volada

Starling, take wing and go.
Tomorrow in the morning, o
you'll go for me
to a far country
where I thought to have a lover.
Find her
and see her.
This is why you're going there:
confront her first
then ask her
why she has turned liar.

I don't know.
It may be
she's bewitched in such a way
she can be loved
but can't love me.
Now, a single meeting would, as
they say, make the morning good,
if she'd grant it me.
A month, I swear,
of her company
is worth any body else's three.

But her strong point easily is
reason, gilded till it blinds.
And when it comes to falsity
she *is* a find.
Trust her? You'll go crazy.
And watch out for her dice,
they're loaded and she uses them.
Know it and watch out.

Seems to me
she's more crafty

than an old fox, speak of hunting.
Lately she kept me all night baying
   until day.
   Her desires
   are capricious,
   tricky too.
Even kids'll make songs for you
   on her faithlessness.

He must have been enchanted, him
   where her love was given.
There ha'nt been such a catechism
   since Elias was a pup.
      Fly!
   get there, hurry up!
Tell her I'll die if I don't know
   if she sleeps
   nightshirt or raw!

Her beauty was born with her, without perfume of cress or herbs. But!
shacked up with a thousand lovers!
mistress of a thousand lords!
   And Marcabrus
   says her house
   is not closed.
She quits the one who wants her most.
   He gawks and gapes
   now that use
has put an end to rubbing.

            Love considered
            and desired,
         her furry little flower is
            better put,
            bless the slut,
         than it is with any other.

The present speaker,
a small fool,
will commit great folly soon.
I pardon even the benevolence
of the abbot
of St. Privat,
believing without malevolence
that if we play out this game
and she calls "MATE"
love'll come down like rain.

The disloyalty
she has done me
I make it even
pay her back
and give myself to her, the devil.
But under me
she'll have to be on the level,
and then hug me
and then nip me . . .

Ges l'estornels non s'oblida

The starling didn't loaf around,
didn't even stop to eat, but
when he had the message straight
he didn't wait for a thing. He
        took wing
        flew so hardy,
        made the effort,
        hunted round
        did this birdie,
        hurdy-gurdy,
        found her out
        and began to sing.

                On a flowered branch he sat,
                this gay bird and cried and spit,
                        cleared his throat
                        and sang again.
                Finally she got the point.
                        Casement opened
                        when she pushed it,
                        he got poised:
                        —I'm a bird, he said.
                        "Fine," said she.
                        "Kindly tell me
                        what's your racket?
                        Why're you making so
                much noise, or what love sent you?"

                —Beyond Lerida, said the starling,
                you've broken so many lances, darling,
                with cavaliers, I cannot answer
                liars who besmirch your credit.
                        A thousand lovers
                        flatter themselves,
                        one and all.

49

Your friend the abbot
taking profit
from your hospitality
takes the credit
for your fall.

"The abbot undertook invasion
without having my permission.
And since he stirred no love in me
and I am not his guarantee, I
think I call my will my own.
        I love another
        want him here.
        As for disa-
        greeable boobies,
        they get ousted
        on their ear.
I give my disdain no cover.

"One-sided, and my love is sworn.
If he wills it I consent—bird,
go tell him, tell him nice, till
now he's slept on a block of ice
        compared with me.
        AND that he
        gives me leisure,
        and in my lack
        I think of inviting
        the abbot back.

"Where the ceiling is the night
there's a rich pleasure to enjoy;
soft kisses from her who already
feels his weight in her delight.
        Okay starling?
        Go and say
        that tomorrow

break of day,
if he'll be
under that tree,
we'll make end,
I under him,
of all this bad feeling."

With the mission neatly ended,
the starling glided, hardly winded,
to his master came and cried :
—You have a lady of great worth!
The thousand lovers
she has greeted
with a thousand greetings only;
put their beards
to gorgeous spreads
without according
what you feared . . .
that the spread was on the bed.

—She charged me
to tell you
to be there where she said.
She'll be there
in the garden
and'll mate you. Sirs, the end!

Al departir del brau tempier

At the point of separating out
of harsh weather,
when it begins to soften,
the sap rising along the branches
sap that revives
furze and heather
and turns the peach tree to a mess of blossom,
the frogs sing from the marshes, and
willow and elder
lengthen,
I intend now to make a vers against
the months of dryness.

I think of a great orchard
small handsome trees all through it;
noble graftings, well-fleshed fruit
(perhaps too fleshy—
one would expect the worst?)
They put forth leaf and apple flower, which
when fruit comes
prove to be willow and elder.
When the head is empty
afflicted are tips and branches.

The good first growth is dead. Those that survive
are but twigs and rushes.
Brave enterprises, they defect, I see it,
eager though to show their skill at dancing;
prodigious, swaggering promises, but
as for fruit
empty as elder and willow,
so that we call them flabby, irksome, dull,
I and all other hirelings and soldiers.

When they are all night around the fire,
Sire Esteve, Sir Constans and Sir Hugh,
raising bids to outvaunt one another,
more gallant than Berard de Monleydier,
all night they tilt and wrassle in their pints.
At dawn
in the shadow of the elder,
you'll hear the row and wrangling, their disputes
as they double bets again.
Their game of checkers.

Damned blackguards and blockheads, these boobs-gone-bad,
can't even imitate what their fathers did.
Towns like Cazeres and Sarlouch
you'd say are worth Montpellier? and Toulouse?
I know what deaths their fathers had—
made for themselves!
And the best of these bushes is an elder.
You can say he would be damned lucky
to look and find among them olive and laurel.

Even the gardner and the turnkey go, flee, eyes
closed, as if wind blew them out.
These later scions have made a villainous swap:
for smock and clogs
they leave fine britches and their cloaks of vair,
there's nothing to gain from the new locataire.
All that they can raise in way of fire
is my anger!
These willows and elders . . .
if they weren't backed up by kings or counts or dukes
they'd be plain vags, roadmen, thieves, con-men.

God aid the valiant who have their price entire,
for these malevolent rich appear as elders—

one reason the world's a mixed-up stupid mess
   that grubs
          and rots
               and vegetates
in its own disease.

LAUDATOR   •   TEMPORIS   •   ACTI

MARCABRU

En abriu s'esclairo il riu contra'l Pascor

In April around Easter the streams grow clear
and in the groves, leaves burgeon above the blossoms.
Gentle, with gentle pleasure, gently
Pure Love comforts me.

Who has an acknowledged lover of one sort
should take him as white if he be not rubbed dark:
pied love, always, the best I can see it
being traitor from habit.

Pretends it's good bettering itself, gently
serving, while evil is what it's after. When
favor's given you'll see the heads broken
in many places, and muddied reputations.

God down and damn eternally pied love and curse forever
all it stands for! The drunk at least takes pleasure
in his letch—though if he drink too much
it drains his vigor.

If my love will disbelieve the muck that liars
make and snakes construct, my garrulous accusers,
I'll be hers if she wants me,
without loud-talk or falsity,
without lies or illusions.

But she doesn't believe me. I waste my time
reproaching her without a belt.
She makes her peace with hell and helling:
so the tongue turns toward the swelling
tooth, where the pain is felt.

Three of them pass before where I sit in the passage: I'm silent
until the fourth has finished fucking her and the fifth

comes tearing up.
That's where Amor is now, in foulness and filth. These cunts

are nymphos in bed
seducers when they talk
and thieves when they sleep,
and these male sluts not only want their piece—
but some back in theirs as well, and the best thing!
how shepherds make it with a sheep...ka..
how describe this "culture"?
He takes the skin off a hard bird, who flays
and skins a vulture...

Per savi'l tenc ses doptansa

No doubt at all,
I'll take him on as critic,
who'll call the meaning, in my song,
of each word,
who's analytic, who
can see the structure of the vers unfold.
I know it'll sound absurd, but
I'm often doubtful and go wrong myself
in the explication of an obscure word.

These simple-minded troubadours get off
on tangents which have the excellent merit
of leading nowhere.
And they turn into compulsion what
plain truth has accorded them.
Out of what truth has set in order, they
make compulsory laws
and by a certain reflection
they fit their words to fill the chinks and flaws.

Without demarcation
they set Love and the several ways
of letching-after-love on equal footing.
And he who's on the make for simple bedding
will find it is himself he covers up.
When his purse is empty as a street in winter
he'll see the sport of sledding hard
will serve for consolation.

I get sore and I show it, when I hear
from some poor sonofabitch that Love
has misled and betrayed him, when
it's lechery has thrown him out.
It's to themselves such lovers lie,

for a lover's treasure
is in measure, patience, and in Joy.

Some couplings make known
when two paths join and do not redivide,
that of two desires, one
will may be made,
and Fine Love walk beside
and live and stay
where trust lives, within
the honest loving whiteness of their days.

For Love has the sign
of emerald and sard,
is Joy's peak and basis,
and of Truth, the teacher,
and has power over
every creature.

To judge from the semblance
when he speaks acts, Love
arises from the heart of things
when he lays down his gage and does
not qualify his giving for a rule.
The man who does not advance
straitly toward Love
's a fool.

But it is not worth an egg, my preaching at him, whose
already miserable heart is strapped by madness.
For I, too, think that sensual love
proceeds from the affections,
although too often it proves false and thieving.

The fool sings out everything he has in mind.
He follows no intelligence but
tinkers the job and botches it:

his love lives on a kind of extortion,
his life is a constant makeshift.
I agree on principle, then: love
loves itself,
constantly is steadfast,
and probity has sliminess for breakfast.

The end of this vers uncoils against
and sets the weights to balance
this vicious, villainous crew of mutts
whose stars are red with malice,
who puff themselves up with crazy thoughts
and have great adventures summarily,
that is, they decide to have them . . .

May the thought that inflates them
bring them bad luck only.

L'iverns vai e'l temps s'aizina

Winter goes and weather betters,
hedgerows green, hawthorns flower,
for which sensible reason the birds rejoice.

Even man grows gray with love
each drawing toward his private choice
   yeah,
pursuing his heart's pleasure.

The cold and drizzle clink against
the gentle season to arrest it.
From the hedges and from thickets
I hear the lancing song contest it.

Put down my name in the entry-books,
I'll sing of Love and how it goes,
   yeah,
if I want to, *and* how it grows.

Letching love gets started, then it grabs
and cheats with a greedy, dire will.
Had just once, a cunt's softness
combusts, lights the damned traitorous fire.

And no one who falls into that blaze,
if he really mean it, or just to try it
   yeah,
will come out with his hair on Fridays.

Fine Love carries a medicine
intended to heal his companion.
Lechery binds and cramps his well
then shoves him down into a kind of hell.

Long as there's the smell of money
it'll wear love's face both front and rear
    yeah,
    but when the cash runs low, you'll hear
    "the road, sonny, the road."

Luring, enticing with sweet bait
to get the poor gull into the trap
until they have him, head and shoulders,
signal "yes" while saying "no":

I prefer as lover a man who's dark
or light-skinned, or nicely tanned,
I'll make it with you—no I won't
    yeah,
    crazy for a skinny behind!

The lady doesn't know Love's face
when she loves a servant of the house:
and if he covers her at her will
then it's the mongrel with the greyhound bitch.

That's how these rich alloys are got
who will not lay out feasts or silver
    yeah,
    and it's Marcabru who says so.

The guardian gets into the back
and hurries to blow up the fire a bit,
then drinks the smoke from the waterbutt
of his Lady Goodandexcited.

I know how well he rests when he lies down
    and gets the grain out of the sack
    yeah,
    and perpetuates his master's name.

Who has Amor as a neighbor
and lives on the allowance he gets,
good name, spunk and integrity
incline to him without complaint.

He who acts as straight as he talks
will not have the same laments as
     yeah,
Sir Eglain, that balancing grain-sack.

For myself, I hold no more
with Sir Eble's theory of *trobar*
that's made a stack of foolish decisions
and upholds them against all reason.

I say, and've said, and will again:
they feed us only rationalization.
Love weeps to be differentiated
from lechery. Plain, it's plain
that he who whines against Fine Love
     's a botch. Let him complain
          yeah.

Dirai vos en mon lati

I'll tell you
in my own way
what I've seen
and what I see.
I think the world will hardly last
according to scripture, for nowadays
the son fails toward the father,
father toward son equally.

Youth, turned from the road toward full decline
    and Gift, who was his brother,
    slip off in the night together.
And our Sir Constans, the Great Deceiver,
    would never have missed them.

Often, a rich man's bread and wine
feed a bad neighbor, and if he
has a hard face, it's sure to be
a hard morning, if what the farmer
    says is true,
or that's how the proverb goes.

In the mill, the miller judges:
"What's well bound should be well loosed."
And the labourer behind his plowshare:
"Good harvest comes from a good field"
"Evil son from evil mother"
"The likerous mare breeds a mean-
    hearted little beast."

Two colts are born—mettlesome, handsome,
with blond manes that will turn from
blond to mouse and make them resemble two asses.
Youth and Joy have turned into swindlers
    and Malice sent in as replacement.

You married men, you act like goats.
You plump the cushions up a bit,
the cunts all wink and get undressed.
But it cuts both ways—and when you say

"My sons laugh at me"
and you've had nothing to do with it,
that is, the birth of your sons, what goats!
You have a spirit that would look better sheepish.
Worth nothing to me to lecture at 'em.
The errors they make are always the same.
And one thing Marcabru's never seen,
and that's these merry married men
    give up their cheating
    when love's the game.

Always you cut instead of shaving, lads,
    when love's the game.

Pus mos coratges s'es clartits

Since my courage is clarified
by the Joy I'm given, and I
see Love parcel out and choose,
wherein I hope to be a richness to her,
I do a good job and winnow out my song
so no one can put me in the wrong,
since for a little thing
a man can be contradicted when he sings.

> The one whom Fine Love singles out
> lives happy, courteous and wise.
> And he to whom Joy is refused, is
> undone, sent out to ruin. For he
> who carps at Love is made to hang
> his mouth wide like a fool and think
> it was his own artifice destroyed him.

> Such are false-hearted judges, thieves,
> false-witnesses and cheating husbands,
> back-biters, painted-up young men,
> lip-servicers and convent-crackers,
> and these flaming whores who'll do
> agreeable things with other women's
> husbands, all will earn their hell.

Homicides, traitors, the crud that sells
church preferments, the magicians,
usurers, in sex the aestheticians
who make livings from their dirty trade,
those who submit themselves to charms
and the fetid hags who make them, will
all share unrelenting flames.

Seducers, drunkards, false priests, false
abbots, nuns, the false recluse

will get theirs then, says Marcabru.
For each one has his seat reserved,
Fine Love has promised it will be thus:
great lamentation and gnashing teeth.

O noble Love, source of all giving,
by whom the whole world is illumined,
I cry mercy!
Keep these whiners from me! and
may I be defended against the fire!
On every side I hold myself your prisoner,
and comforted by you in all things, hope
that you shall be my guide and all my light.

With this vers I curb my heart
and direct the reproach at myself,
for he who would be a critic
is in, if he can guard himself, not
blot himself with the same crime
he charges the lady with, and think
he's in the right to rate her down.

And if it is a well-chosen bit,
what I know to say well, and say,
he can if he like, remember it.

JAUFRÉ RUDEL DE BLAIA

(middle 12th C.)

VIDA

Jaufré Rudel was a very noble man, the prince of Blaia. He fell in love with the countess of Tripoli without ever having seen her, on the strength of the glowing descriptions he had of her from pilgrims travelling from Antioch. He made many good verses for her, but with poor words, though the tunes were good. And because of his desire to see her, he took the cross and put to sea.

He took sick on board the vessel, and at Tripoli they thought he was dead and carried him to an inn. When it was known to the countess, she came to him, to his bed, and took him in her arms. And he knew that she was the countess and immediately recovered his sense of hearing and smell, and he praised God that he had sustained his life until he had seen her. Then he died in her arms.

She did him the highest honors, having him buried in the house of the Templars; and on the same day she became a nun because of the grief she had at his death.

Lanquan li jorn son lonc en mai

When the days are long in May
it's good,
soft birdsong from afar,
and when the melody leaves me
I remember my love afar.
I've been bent and thoughtful with desire until
hawthorn flowers & all that song
mean no more to me than snow in winter.

I believe that the gods know
and want
me to see my love afar:
but for every good coming my way
my bad luck doubles, that she is far.
I'd gladly be a pilgrim, if my
grim cape and staff might fall within the
compass of her eye!

Joy'd come to me then, when I cry God's name
begging my shelter afar.
But I don't know when I shall see her
and our lands are wide apart, far.
For though there are roads and trails enough
I am sure of nothing. May't
go as God wills it.

I'll never have joy of Love if it
come not
from this love afar.
Better? Lovelier? I know of none
in any place, either near or far.
Her price so pure, I'd rather be
a captive prince held by the bloody Saracens
to be near her.

God, who made all that walk or stir,
and made me
for this love afar,
give me the power of the desire I have
to look on my love afar
truly, and in such fine haven, that a simple room
a simple garden
'll seem a palace seen in dream.

He calls me truly who says I letch
desirous of this love afar.
No other joy could mean so much
as that I have
my love afar.
But what I want so is forbid, spell's thrown
and now I'm bound to love,
to be loved
never.

I'm kept from her I want so much.
And damn for
ever, him who threw the
curse that spells me, bids me love
forever,
loved, never.

Quan lo rius de la fontana

When, from the spring, the stream
   runs clear, so in Spring
     sun clears the air,
     eglantine appears.
  The nightingale in brake
modulates, clarifies his song,
    softens it, reiterates,
   polishes and sweetens it :
only right that I my own song soften.

My distant love, for you, my
     whole body aches:
and I can find nothing to heal it
     but in your call
     that has as bait
  soft love behind curtain or
in orchard with the mate
    I long for.

That chance refused me forever, it's
    no wonder I burn.
There never was fairer lady, God
    couldn't want one,
Christian, Jewess, or Saracen.
The man who wins even a part of her love
    is fed on manna.

No end to my body's desire toward
    her I love most.
I'm afraid my will will cheat me, over-
    take me with lust;
for that pain is sharper than thorns and cured
    only with joy.
I want pity from no one for a pain
    I would share with no man.

JAUFRÉ RUDEL

tornada

This vers, sung in plain occitan,
we send by Filhol without parchment brief
to Uc le Brun: and happy to know
that everyone, the Poitevins,
the people of Berri and Guyenne
and all the way up to Bretagne
may be happy because of him.

BERNART DE VENTADORN

(c. 1150—1180)

VIDAS

I.

Bernart of Ventadour was from the Limousin, from the castle of
Ventadour. Of poor birth, he was the son of a servant who was a
baker, and who heated the oven and cooked bread for the castle.
Bernart grew to be handsome, courteous, and learned, and was a
skillful man who knew how to sing and compose well. The viscount of Ventadour, his lord, enjoyed having him around, took
great pleasure in his composing and singing, and gave him high
honors.

And the viscount of Ventadour had a pretty wife, young, noble,
and lively. She was pleased with en Bernart and with his songs, and
she fell in love with him and he with her, until he made all his cansos and vers of her, of the love he had with her, and of the lady's
merit.

Their love went on for a long time before the viscount and the people noticed it. When the viscount perceived that it was so, he cooled toward en Bernart and had his wife put under lock and key. He made the lady dismiss en Bernart, something to the effect that he go away and stay away.

And he left. He went to the duchess of Normandy [Eleanor of Aquitaine] who was young and of great merit, understood worth and honor, and cared for a song of praise. Indeed, Bernart's cansos and vers pleased her well, so that she received him in honor, gave him welcome, and made great pleasure for him.

He stayed for a long time in her court and was in love with her and she with him, and he made many good cansos to her. But King Henry of England married her, took her away from Normandy and with him to England. En Bernart stayed behind here, sad and in misery, coming to the good count Raimon of Toulouse where he stayed until the count's death. And when the count died, en Bernart left the world, trobar, singing, and worldly pleasure, entered the order of Dalon, and there he died.

And I, Uc de St. Circ, whatever I have written of him was recounted to me by the viscount Ebles de Ventadour, son of the viscountess en Bernart had loved. And he made these cansos which you will hear written below.

II.

Bernart de Ventadorn was from the Limousin, from the castle Ventadorn, of humble parentage, the son of a servant and a lady-baker, according to Peire d'Alvernhe in his song where he speaks badly of all the troubadours:

> The 3rd is Bernart de Ventadorn
> and a hand shorter than Bornelh.
> He had a good servant in his father
> who used to pull a laburnam bow.
> The old man carried down the wood
> and his mother heated the oven up.

Improving on Bernart's lineage, God gave him a handsome, charming body and a noble heart, which is the beginning of nobility, and gave him wit, knowledge, courtesy, and fine speech; and he had subtlety and the art of finding good words and gay tunes.

He fell in love with the viscountess of Ventadorn, his lord's wife. God gave him such great luck that, because of his handsome bearing and gay songs, she loved him beyond measure, for she did not guard her sense or her nobility, her honor, her worthiness, nor her oath, but her wits went and her will followed them, as Arnaut de Mareuil says:

> thinking of joy, madness forgot,
> my sense fled
> and my will followed it out.

or, as Guy d'Ussel:

> it happens with fine love in such
> a way that sense
> can have no power against desire.

En Bernart was prized and honored by all good people, and his songs gratefully received and honored. He was lionized and welcomed everywhere. Great men and great barons honored him and gave him expensive gifts, so that he traveled in fine clothes and with a fine reputation.

Their love lasted for a long time, until her husband, the viscount, perceived it. And when he noticed it, he was very aggrieved and sad, and made the viscountess, his wife, even more aggrieved and sad. He made her dismiss en Bernart and send him away from that place.

And he left. He went up to Normandy to the duchess who at that time ruled the Normans, who was young and gay and of great valor and price, as well as powerful, and attentive to prestige and honor. She received him honorably and with much pleasure. Being very happy at her conquest, she made him lord and master of her whole court. So, he who had loved his lord's wife fell in love with the duchess and she with him. For a long time he had great joy of her and great happiness, until she married King Henry of England who took her across the Channel. En Bernart never saw her again or heard any message from her.

Then because of the pain and sadness he had from her, en Bernart became a monk and entered the abbey of Dalon, and here he stayed until the end.

RAZO

... and en Bernart called her "La Lauzeta," the Lark, because of a cavalier who loved her; and she called him [Bernart probably, not the nameless knight] "Rai," Sunray. And one day the knight came to the duchess and entered the chamber of the lady. He took the collar of the cloak (lying there) and swung it around his neck, and his own he let fall in its place. Bernart soon saw it, for one of the ladies' maids pointed it out to him covertly. And for this reason he made the canso which goes:

Can vei la lauzeta mover

When I see the lark stir her wings for joy
against the sunlight,
              forgetting herself,
              letting herself
              fall
with the sweetness that comes into her heart,
AIE!
so great an envy comes on me to see her rejoicing
I wonder that my heart does not melt with desiring.

Hell, I
who thought I knew so much of love,
              know so little:
and cannot keep from loving her whose favors
              I shall not have. And she
has all my heart and all myself and all herself and
              all the world, has
robbed my heart from me and left me
              not a thing but my desire
              and a desiring heart.

              It having been granted me,
                       permission,
              having been allowed my moment to look
                       into her eyes,
              since I saw reflected in those eyes
                       my image / that
              image has held the power, not myself!
              Since that mirage, my glass, influx of breath
                       ravages my innards:
              Narcissus at the spring, I kill
              this human self.

Really, though, without hope over the ladies;
never again trust myself to them.

I used to be their champion but
                now I quit them entire. Not
one of them helps me against her who
                destroys and confounds me,
fear and disbelieve all of them,
                all the same cut.

And in this my lady appears very much a woman
                for which I reproach her.
She thinks one should not want what is forbidden him.
                It happens. And here
I have fallen in bad grace,
I have acted like the fool on the bridge.
I don't know why it happens to me unless
I climb too hard against the mountain.

The chance for grace has been lost, I shall not taste it,
for she who should have it most has hardly any, and
                where else shall I seek it?
It is bitter for me to look on her
who lets a helpless wretch die of his desire
                and will not aid him.
                He will have nothing without her.

But I have no right, and no pity or prayer
                can avail me with my lady:
since my loving does not please her, I shall
                speak no more to her of it,
so take my leave, sever myself from her, she
                has killed me,
                answer her like a corpse, she
                does not keep me,
go away into exile, I
                don't even know where.

                Tristans, you'll have no more of me.
                I'm going away with my misery,

don't know where.
I'm giving up my songs and
going off to hide
from all love, from all joy.

BERNART DE VENTADORN

Chantars no pot gaire valer

It is worthless to write a line
if the song proceed not from the heart:
nor can the song come from the heart
if there is no love in it.

Maligning fools, failing all else, brag,
but love does not spoil,
but countered by love, fills,
    fulfilling grows firm.
A fool's love is like verse poor in the making,
only appearance and the name having,
for it loves nothing except itself, can
            take nothing of good,
            corrupts the rhyme.

And their singing is not worth a dime
whose song comes not from the heart.
If love has not set his roots there
the song cannot put forth shoots there: so
my song is superior, for I turn to it
mouth   eyes   mind   heart
and there is the joy of love in it.
And the binding glance is food for it
and the barter of sighs is food for it
and if desire is not equal between them
there is no good in it.

God grants me no strictness to counter my desire
yet I wonder if we afford its acceptance,
responsible for what we have of it. Though
            each day goes badly for me.
Fine thought at least will I have from it
            though no other thing:
for I have not a good heart and I work at it,
a man with nothing.

Yet she has made me rich, a man with nothing.
Beautiful she is and comely, and the more
I see her openness and fresh body, the more
                    I need her and have smarting.
Yet so seldom her fine eyes look on me
one day must last me a hundred.
                    Yet her fine body—
when I gaze on it, I
grow like a canso, perfect.
And, if desire is equal between us
and the darkness enters my throat?

BEATRITZ DE DIA

(second half of the 12th C.)

VIDA

The countess of Dia was the wife of William of Poitou and a good and beautiful lady. She was in love with Raimbaut d'Aurenga and made him many good songs.

BEATRITZ DE DIA

Estat ai en greu cossirier

I have been in heavy thought
over a cavalier I'd had.
I want it clear to everyone
that I've loved him to excess,
and now I see he's left me: pretext, I refused him my love.
I seem to be mistaken, then,
as to what was going on,
dressed or in bed.

I'd love to hold my cavalier
naked one evening in my arms,
he would think he were on fire
if I'd be his pillow then.
For I burn more for him than
Floris did for Blancheflor,
deliver him my love, my heart, my
sensuality, my eyes, my life.

My dear and lovely friend, if ever
I come to have you in my power
and get into bed with you one night
and give you love-kiss, know it:
I'd have such a great desire
to hold you in my husband's place,
if you'd promise me to do
everything I'd want you to.

PEIRE D'ALVERNHE

(c. 1158—1180)

VIDA

Peire d'Auvergne was from the Bishopric of Clermont. He was an intelligent man and well-lettered, the son of a bourgeois, handsome and charming in his person. He composed and sang well, and was the first good troubadour there was beyond the mountains. He made the best tunes for vers that were ever made, and the vers which goes:

During the short days
and the long nights.

He did not make cansos, for there was no singing then called cansos, just vers; for en Giraut de Borneill made the first canso that was ever made. He was much honored and appreciated by all the worthy barons there were at that time, and by all the worthy ladies, and was reputed to be the best troubadour in the world until Giraut de Borneill came along. He praised himself a lot in his songs and criticized the other troubadours, so that he says of himself in one cobla of a sirventes that he made:

> Peire d'Alvernhe has the sort of voice
> which can sing both high and low:
> his tunes are sweet and delightful,
> but then he is master of all, provided
>   he makes his words clear
> for hardly anyone understands them.

For a long time he stayed and lived in the world with the Catharists, according to the Dauphin of Auvergne, who was born in his time; and then he did penance and died.

Chantarai d'asquestz trobadors

My tune is of troubadours who sing variously,
and the worst believes he chants nobly.
I wish they would go somewhere else:
    two hundred shepherds
    trying to pipe
and not a damn one knows whether the tune
    rises or descends.

Peire Rogier sins at this horribly.
To deliver my first indictment, he
    sings too openly of love,
though in church is worth more than a hymn book,
for besides he can carry a candlestick, with
    a large burning candle.

And the second, Giraut de Bornelh,
a wineskin dried in the sun:
his song scratchy and thin, he
has a voice like a water-vendor.
If he ever looked in a mirror
he'd stop singing altogether.

Bernart de Ventadorn is the third
and a hand shorter than Bornelh.
He had a good servant in his father
who could pull a laburnam bow.
His mother heated the oven up, and
brought down the brushwood herself.

        The fourth is from Briva, a Limousin,
        and a shabbier joglar you will not find
            from here to Benevento.
        He sings so like a sick pilgrim I once heard
            that pity
            nearly overtakes me.

Guillem de Ribas (number 5
and surely the meanest man alive)
not content with being a thorough villain
must speak his verses hoarsely.
Such grum sounds a crow would not admit to
and his eyes resemble two aspirin.

And the sixth, Grimoart Gausmars,
a knight on the road as a joglar.
The lord makes a poor trade who grants that one
    bright green clothing.
He would have himself rigged so uniquely
a hundred others would take to the road.

Peire Bermon abased himself when
the count of Toulouse gave him what
he could not graciously ignore:
        wherefore
he was noble to him who despoiled him.
He missed a good chance not cutting off
what the man carries hanging.

Number Eight, Bernart de Saissac, rises
no higher in the profession
than to go about asking donations.
I prize him something less than a garlic
since he begged from Bertrans de Cardalhac
    a sweaty old cloak.

And the ninth, is en Raimbautz
who makes his trobar too proud.
Him I consider a cipher.
Thus we appraise these pipers
who go about asking alms.

Ebles de Sagna, the tenth, o,
love never came gently to him

so he sings as if with a toothache:
a pustular, petulant lawyer.
They say that for two deniers he
will hire himself out in one place, sell
advice par excellence in another.

The eleventh is Guossalbo Roitz
who fills his trobar with conceit.
In him, chivalry has ended its life.
He has never yet struck a fair blow.
While in flight one night, though,
he invented a fierce reputation.

The twelfth is an ancient Lombard
who's always shouting his neighbors are cowards
—meanwhile, he shivers in terror. But
he'll make a bold tune with bastard words,
neither Limousin nor Lombard.
They say he's a charming fellow.

Peire d'Alvernhe has that kind of voice
which can sing both high and low:
his tunes are sweet and delightful, but
then, he is master of all, provided
    he makes his words clear
for hardly anyone understands them.

This vers has been made to bagpipes
at Puivert, laughing and joking.

ARNAUT DE MAREUIL

(last third of the 12th C.)

VIDA

Arnaut de Mareuil was from the bishopric of Périgord, from a castle called Mareuil, and was a clerk of poor extraction. Because he could make no living from his education, he went out into the world, for he was intelligent and knew trobar well. The stars and his luck led him to the court of the countess of Burlatz who was the daughter of the valorous count Raimon and the wife of the viscount of Beziers who was named Talliafero.

This Arnaut was a very handsome and well-built man, sang well and read in the vernacular. And the countess was very good to him, granting him favors and honor. He fell in love with her and made cansos for her, but did not dare to tell her, or anyone else, the name of the one who had written them. He said, rather, that someone else had made them.

But as it happened, love forced him so hard that he made a canso, the one that begins:

La franca captenensa

and in this canso he reveals to her the love that he had for her. The countess did not discourage him, but heard and accepted his pleas and found them agreeable. She outfitted him with some handsome clothes, granted him great honor, and gave him the boldness he needed to compose for her. He came to be a highly respected man in the court and made many good cansos for the countess, which songs disclose that he had great good of her and great pain.

RAZO

You have heard who Arnaut de Mareuil was, and how he was enamored of the countess of Béziers, who was daughter of the good count Raimon de Toulouse and mother of that viscount of Béziers whom the French murdered when they had taken Carcassonne. The aforesaid viscountess was called the countess of Burlatz because she was born in the castle of Burlatz. Arnaut was very affected by her and made many good cansos for her, and begged her with great timidity that she love him.

King Anfos, who was in love with the countess, noticed that she looked well on Arnaut de Mareuil, and was extremely jealous when he saw the loving semblances with which she favored him. He heard the fine cansos he had made to her and reproached her with Arnaut, spoke so much to her and had many other people mention it to her, that she rebuked Arnaut and dismissed him. She forbade him to come into her presence or to make any cansos of her, and insisted that he leave, that he cease entreating her and withdraw his love.

When he heard the dismissal in this way, Arnaut de Mareuil was grieved beyond all complaining, and left her and her court like a man without any hope at all.

Where he went was to en Guillen de Montpellier, who was his lord and friend. He stayed with him for a long while, and in Montpellier he moaned and there he wept and there also he made the canso which goes:

Molt eron dous mei consir

which canso is written so, as you will hear.

Bel m'es quan lo vens m'alena

The wind is fair
that flows upon me
late in April before May starts up.
And nightingale and jay sing
                        against the crickets
                        the whole peaceful night.
Each bird announces his joy without restraint
                        in his own language
                        in the morning freshness
settles down with his mate.

All earthly things rejoice the birth of leaves :
nor can I help remembering the love in which
                        I rejoice.
            By usage and by nature I
                                    turn toward joy
                        like any other single creature;
                        there where the soft wind blows
                                    my heart goes,
                                    revives.

Whiter than Helen,
lithe in gracefulness,
more than the fresh-opened flower is fair
                        she is fair;
                                    white teeth,
                                    true words,
                                    open-hearted,
                                    without trickery,
            clear complexion and auburn hair—
O God, who grants her this seignory, preserve her,
for one more lovely than she is I have never seen.

If she does not prolong the dispute
I shall count myself blessed,

instead were to give me to start with
a kiss,
and so forth,
according to my length of service.
For then
we shall make a short journey often
down a short path,
since her fine body
has set me readily
in this course.

Bel m'es lo dous temps amoros

Lovely to look at,
this soft green world I rejoice in and
grow glad within
the simple joy of new flowers
                                    and sing
of love where hope's the pin.
                    I'm in my body morning and night
and nowhere see a worry or sad thought.

                    Lovely to look at,
                    so she is,
the lady where my intention is fixed. Her
name is high and good, for in her beauty,
                                    valor pleases,
                                    reflecting the other,
                                    never mixed,
which makes me even more timid and ill at ease.
            The best shouldn't fall to me,
            and when I look upon it, the
most terrible longings and desires increase.

            She
scarce leaves my thought
for in my world
nothing else pleases so much.
Good if she lead me wrong!
Good if she kill me!
since she has set me forever in love.
If she humble me terribly to her,
                                    at her pleasure,
if I die each day and cannot move me from her,
I say, rather, the solace of martyrs refreshes.

Then, if this sweet ill is good in my sight,
                                    I need some solace

that she cure me of it.
If she to whom I submit would aid, deliver me—
Sweet God of Love!
will you do something for me?
Accomplish my desire, it's in your see, try, try,
try to turn her fancy some small whit toward me!

If only there were news that she
would be undressed one evening there for me,
if only I could serve her
please, I could not want for greater gain.
If she made her presence to the proof of knowing
I'd be insane
to take any solace thereafter.
Hands' games have there
what's value more than laughter.

'Gainst tricky talkers,
filth on their mouths destroying love.
Each lover should take cover and conceal his heart,
for that such are
false takes time to prove. Let
the world consider the attitude factitious, one
should hardly ever tell the truth outright—how?
when the lies and excuses are more effective.

The vers I send to my lady for her pleasure.
I make it badly.
Run! How refrain
when I speak to you of her from
swift intake of breath?

ARNAUT DANIEL

(c. 1180—1210)

VIDA

Arnaut Daniel was from the same region as Arnaut de Mareuil, the bishopric of Périgord, from a castle called Ribeyrac. He was wellborn, took well to letters, and had great delight in composing.

Abandoning letters he became a joglar and took to a way of composing with difficult rhymes, for which reason his songs are neither easy to understand or to learn.

He loved a noble lady of Gascoigne, the wife of en Guillem de Buovilla, but it was not believed that the lady granted him pleasure in the matter of love, because he says:

> I am Arnaut who gathers wind,
> who hunts with the ox to chase a hare
> forever, and strives upstream
> against the current.

RAZO

It happened that he was at the court of King Richard of England. While he was there another joglar challenged him, claiming that he composed with rhymes more difficult than Arnaut's. Arnaut took it as a joke and they made their bets (each his horse), which they placed under the power of the king. And the king shut each of them up in separate rooms.

En Arnaut was so bored he couldn't bind one word to another. The joglar, though, made his song easily and quickly. They had first ten days' space, and then only five before the songs were to be judged before the king. The joglar asked Arnaut if he had made it, and Arnaut said "Yes, three days ago," and he hadn't even begun to think of it.

The joglar practiced all night singing his song in such a way that you could hear it very well. And Arnaut thought of how to pull a trick: there came a night when the joglar was singing it, and en Arnaut went and memorized the whole tune.

They came before the king. Arnaut said he would like to recite his canso, and started off very well on the song the joglar had made. The joglar when he heard that looked Arnaut straight in the face and said that he had made it. King Richard asked how that could be. The joglar begged the king to hear the vers. Richard asked Arnaut, "Look, what's happening?" And Arnaut confessed to the king how everything had come about. The king was well pleased and thought the whole story very amusing, ordered the bets cancelled, the horses released, and made Arnaut and the joglar each a handsome present. The song was given to Arnaut Daniel, and goes:

Anc yeu non l'ac, mas ela m·a

(She has me, but I still don't have her). And here you will find some of his work.

En cest sonet coind' a leri

On this gay and slender tune
I put and polish words and plane
and when I've passed the file they'll be
             precise and firm.
For Love himself pares down and gilds my song
which moves from her whose glances are
the firm light rails that guide all excellence.

I tell you frankly, she I adore and serve
's the loveliest in the world.
Because I'm hers from head to toe
I cleanse myself, and though wind blow in winter
the love flowing within my heart keeps ice
out of the stream the coldest weather.

I burn oil lamps, wax tapers, no pretense I
hear a thousand masses out for my intention,
that God grant me by his intervention
good success with her against
whom all resistance is useless.
And when I think of her auburn hair, her
merry body, svelte and lissom,
I love her better than if they gave me Lusena.

I love her with fire
             seek her with such
excess of desire
             I feel I float.
Loving without stint one loses weight.
Her heart submerges mine in a great flood that nothing
will evaporate.
She takes such usury of love she'll end
             by owning tavern and bartender.

I do not want the Roman Emp.
nor to be elected pope
if I can't
      turn toward her
      where my heart
is kindled to a blaze nothing can quell.
          The meat
browns and catches fire, flames, cracks and splits,
and if she doesn't heal me with a kiss
before New Year's she destroys me, she
damns me to hell. And I

cannot turn from loving her too well.
The pain I put up with's hard, this
solitude wraps me round and is my theme.
          On this cover
          I embroider
          words for rhymes.
My fate is worse than his who plows a field, for
though my field's a little bit of earth, I love,
I love it better than Mondis loved Audierna.

      I am Arnaut
      who gathers the wind
      who hunts with an ox
      to chase a hare
forever, and swims against the current.

PEIRE VIDAL

(c. 1175—1205)

VIDA

Peire Vidal was from Toulouse, the son of a furrier, and sang better than any man in the world. He was one of the maddest fellows who ever lived, for he believed as truth whatever he wanted or whatever happened to please him. And he succeeded in making his songs lighter than anyone else's, and made richer tunes and greater follies of arms and love. And he was apt to speak badly of others. It was true that a knight of St. Gilles had had his [Vidal's] tongue cut out, having been given to understand that Peire was his wife's lover. Uc del Bauz took care of him then, and had his tongue treated and cured.

When his tongue had healed he went overseas and brought back with him a Greek girl who'd been given to him as wife on Cyprus. He had been told that she was the niece of the emperor of Constantinople, and given to understand that he, having married her, ought by right to have the empire. Whereupon he put everything he could earn into raising a fleet, intending to go conquer the empire.

He went about carrying imperial arms and had his wife called "empress" and himself "the emperor."

He fell in love with all the pretty ladies in sight, and was suitor for all their loves: all told him to do and say whatever he wished, so he believed himself the lover of each of them, and that each was dying for him. All of them deceived him. He was always leading expensive chargers and wearing rich arms, riding with a chair and a tent with imperial insignia. He thought he was the best knight in the world, and the most beloved of the ladies.

RAZOS

I.

Peire Vidal, as I have told you, was in love with all the lovely ladies, and thought that all of them were in love with him. And now, if you like, I'll tell you how he fell in love with a lady, Alazais de Rocamartina, who was the wife of Barrals, lord of Marseille, he who loved Peire Vidal above any man in the world for his rich trobar and for the crazy things that he did and said. They called each other mutually "Rainier" and Peire was closer to the court and chamber of en Barrals than any other man in the world.

Indeed, Barrals knew that Peire was in love with his wife, and considered it a pass-time, as did everyone else there who knew of it. He enjoyed the foolishness that Vidal performed and spoke, and the lady accepted it lightly, as did all the other ladies to whom Peire Vidal made love. And each one of them spoke pleasantly to him, and promised him anything that pleased them as well as everything he asked for. And he was so knowing that he swallowed it all. The lady Alazais allowed him to court her and beg her love because of the fine cansos he made for her, and for the fun she got out of it with him. And she was with him in the court, they dressed like one another, and she presented him with arms. And if Peire Vidal grew angry with her over anything, Barrals immediately made the peace between them, and made her promise him anything he asked for.

Then a day came when Peire Vidal knew that en Barrals had risen early and that the lady was alone in her room. He entered the room and went to the bed of ma domna Alazais and found her sleeping. Kneeling before her, he kissed her on the mouth: she felt the kiss and thought it was Barrals, her husband, and rose laughing. When she looked and saw that it was the mad Vidal, she began to cry out and raised a great clamor. Ladies and girls came running from within when they heard it and asked: "What's this?" Peire Vidal ran out.

The lady sent for her husband and began to tell him how that crazy Peire Vidal had kissed her. And she wanted him to have Vidal killed, and wept and begged him to take his vengeance immediately. Barrals, like the noble and sophisticated person he was, took her and comforted her, and laughed and chided his wife that she had made so much noise over what a fool had done. But he could not chastise her for it, because she might spread the story around, and people would seek and enquire, much to Vidal's harm. So he only made him great threats.

At which point Peire boarded a vessel for Genoa out of fear. He stayed there until he went overseas with King Richard, for he was set in the fear that Alazais would have him seized. And Alazais would have exerted herself more than slightly if she could have found him. In one song he says:

> One sore   I reproach her for,
> she forced me to go overseas
> to rid the region of me,
> at least that's how it looks to me.

And he stayed there for a long time and made many good cansos recalling the kiss he'd stolen. And in one canso called *Ajostar e lassar* he says that he had from her not the slightest reward

> but a small silk cord, and
> there was another thing:
> I entered her house one morning
> and kissed her like a thief
>   chin and mouth.

And elsewhere he says:

> I would have been more honored than any man born,
> had that stolen kiss been granted me
> and given nicely.

And in still another canso, says:

> Love beats me with the sticks I cut myself:
> for one time, in a high and regal room,
> I stole a kiss of which my heart remembers.

He was overseas for a long time for he didn't dare return to Provence. And when they saw this, the barons, en Barrals and Uc des Baux, implored the lady so often that she pardoned him the affair of the kiss and granted it to him as a gift. Barrals sent him letters and greetings, said his vexation was forgotten, and wrote him to come. And Vidal took ship and came back to Provence to Uc des Baux. En Barrals, as soon as he knew that Peire Vidal was at Les Baux, mounted horse and went to him and led him back to Marseille where he was welcomed by Alazais, and she granted him the kiss out of graciousness that he had stolen from her, of which Peire Vidal made the canso which starts:

> Since I have returned to Provence

in which he says:

> I have won with a great
> softness, after long waiting,
> that kiss which Love's force
> forced me to snatch from my lady.
> Now she grants it to me and
> finds it pleasing.

II

Peire Vidal was in grief over the death of the good count Raimon de Toulouse, and gave himself over to sorrow. He dressed all in black, cut the ears and tails from all his horses, and even had all his servants shave their heads, though they refused to cut their nails or shave off their beards. He went about for a long time mourning like a madman.

And it happened that, during the time he was going about like that, King Alfons of Aragon came up into Provence: and with him came Blascol Romieus, Garcia Romieus, Martin del Canet and Miguel de Luzia, Sans d'Antilon, Guillem d'Alcalla, Albert de Castelvieil, Raimon Gauserans de Pinons, Guillem Raimon de Moncada, Arnaut de Castelbon, and Raimon de Cerveira. And they found Peire Vidal sad and grieving and in this way dressed like a fool. And the king and all the barons protested that they were his special friends, and asked that he leave off grieving and sing and be happy again, and that he should make them a canso to take back to Aragon. The king and his barons were so insistent, he said yes he would, put off sorrow and rejoice and make a canso and do whatever else might please them.

And he loved besides, Loba de Penautier, and ma domna Estefania who was from the Cerdanya. And later he was enamoured of ma domna Raimbauda de Biolh. Biolh is in Provence, in the mountains separating Provence from Lombardy. La Loba was from Carcassonne. Peire Vidal called himself Lop because of her, and carried the badge of wolf. In the mountains of Cabaret, shepherds hunted him with dogs, greyhounds and great mastiffs, as if the man had been a wolf. In fact he wore a wolfskin, giving that scent to the dogs and their masters. And the shepherds hunted him down with the dogs and beat him so badly that he was taken for dead, and carried to the dwelling of Loba de Penautier.

And when she knew that this was Peire Vidal, she was greatly amused at the folly he had committed and began to laugh heartily, and her husband likewise. They accepted him with great joy. Her husband had him carried in and laid in a secret place, while they nursed him as best they could. Then he sent for a physician and had him treated until he was well.

As I'd started to tell you, when he had begun to sing and compose cansos, as he had promised the king of Aragon and his barons, the king had (identical) arms made for himself and for Peire Vidal, had clothes made for the both of them: they dressed alike and the king was highly pleased. Peire Vidal then made this canso which you shall hear, and which begins:

> I had left off singing in grief
> that my lord count had died.

Plus que·l paubres que jatz e·l ric ostal

MORE THAN A BEGGAR I dare not
grumble,
more than a poor man who sleeps in a rich man's hall
who doesn't dare complain
though his complaint be great, fearing
his lord take offense, I
dare not grate against my mortal pain
though having for reason her disdain toward me
whom I've wanted more than any,
at least that!
and yet dare not cry mercy—
I fear so to have her angry at me.

When I look upon her in contemplation my
heart so melts, myself entire forgot,
I stand like a man in ecstasy
before a window where beauty is
resplendant against the sun.
Love beats me with the sticks I cut myself:
one time, in a high and regal room, I
stole a kiss.
My heart remembers it.

That makes it now how many Octobers
the lady I sing upon these pages
has sinned against Love? She
neglects me
does not aid me
still is aware
I've left with her my hope, my heart entire, my love
and have no care
for any other wages.
But why does she signal and welcome me so gently
if she has no intention

of granting me what the lack of which so pains me?
   I'll suffer again
      the things that give me pain.

A man ought, with his rightful lord, to pardon all,
if he be wrong or just, wise or a fool.
A man will put himself to some pains in a war
   to gain honor.
      But when he's exiled from home
        it's hard,
      it takes the fight out of him.
And if I fall away from loving her,
   that's the worst exile, but
      no. I will not.
   I love her now more than before
and she would only contemn me, were
I to smile at fate and leave off loving.
No fear of that,
for all I am and have I have
only through that loving. And

she has me altogether in her puissance,
   can make me suffer all she likes,
      I'll not be bitter.
I have so soft a knowledge to do her pleasure
   I lose the memory of my own
      nor care. No day is
        my love for her does not
      spring, well up from the heart.
   When we're together and I look on her
such a joy rises in me to the eyes that
      putting the horse behind the cart
      my heart
imagines such fine things that in the world there's nothing
else I can
desire or want.

AND SUCH LOVE CUTS THE HEART
FOR I HAVE SEEN NONE more lovely or soft
nor of such bounty. So I have great richness
        loving one who's worth all of it.
    If ever I have the joy to see
    her undressed, alone with me,
I'll be happier than the lord of Excideuil,
who keeps his courage when others but recede.
        I know of none his equal
        saving Geoffrey.

With the four kings of Spain
it all goes badly
since they do not want to make a peace among them—
otherwise it's certain that their valor's great,
        they're frank and loyal
        courteous and straight,
yet, they still might grace their acts
        till they dazzle and gleam,
    if they turned their war to another register
    and fought
the Saracen who call our religion a joke, FIGHT
    until the whole of Spain would be
    united under a single faith.
    A dream.

    Bel-Castiat, my lord, in your account, put
    me down as one who's sad and over-grave.
    The sight of you or Vierna I cannot have
        whom I love
        from the heart and with a single faith.
        A dream.

Ab l'alen tir vas me l'aire

I suck deep in air come from Provence to here.
All things from there so please me
when I hear
in dockside taverns
travelers' gossip told
I listen smiling,
and for each word ask a hundred smiling words,
all news is good

for no man knows so sweet a country as
                    from the Rhône down to Vence.
If only I were locked between
            Durance and the sea!
Such pure joy shines in the sun there.
        I left my heart-for-rejoicing there
            among noble people,
and with her who bids my sadness dance.

No man can ever pass a day in boredom
            who has remembrance of her,
for she is the beginning and birth of all joy:
            and he who would praise her
no matter how well he speaks of her, he lies!
for this world shall not look on one
                better or fairer.

And if there's anything
I know to say or do, I
merit no praise from it,
for in her is all good
and through her I've wit and knowledge of fulfillment,
so am both poet and happy.
And all I make which has in it any fineness
I have from the rich delight of her fine body,
even as my heart longs for her in straightness.

Una canso ai faita mortalmen

One canso I've made murderously,
so much so
I don't know how I did it.
Evening, morning, day or night
I am not master of my thought,
                less of my heart.
            Another time when great
            incertitudes were in the balance-pan,
there came to me from Love so overwhelming a
            proof of my luck,
I began to make a canso on the spot.
            It went like that.

            But why keep me in such a confusion?
She must know that nothing ever pleased me so much.
            From that first hour,
                the first touch,
I could not split my heart, my love, my mind
                away from what I'd found. So
that now if she harms me, it's bound to be
                a disaster for me.
            But if she gives me token
            of accord and friendship, then it's certain
she couldn't offer greater grace or mercy.
And if she need a reason to be right,
            let it
                be that her love sustains me.

But I don't believe at all in her desire, though
she speak and smile and make me promises. No
woman ever lied more agreeably
                or with such cleverness.
            But I can't help believing when she speaks,
on such peak
of ecstasy

her words put me.
But if she speak truth,
not France and I the king of all would make
me feel so happy and peaceful.
But no, she has no heart or good will in the wrangle.

No one ever loved so crazily,
not even he,
the squire who died at table.
I also die
but me she kills more slowly,
and she knows
to do it courteously.
She does not strike with lance or cut with knife
but with soft words and pleasant-seeming welcome.
There you have the weapons she fights me with,
has,
ever since I've known her,
and will
still,
if she keeps me on.

To complete the inventory of her arsenal
I can't forget
beauty, God-given entirely,
nor has he
taken one whit from her:
intelligence, perfect,
perfectly sincere and always gay.
I get this way
because she
does not permit me her love.
Yet they say
one can get fresh water from the sea, which gives me
hope that genius, say, and mind, and
the fact that she does not reject me wholly
will find me Joy someday.

Nothing else can quell
or allay this fire.

Lady cure me, don't
stand and watch me die, a Lazarus,
              of this sweet sickness.
My running away from it's no good,
       my eyes play tricks.
When I leave
I see your beauty before me upon all the roads,
       can neither go
              nor go back.
       May I die accursed in hell
       if I had the whole world, but lacked
you

and things stood well.

PEIRE VIDAL

Tart mi vieran mei amic en Tolosa

It'll be a long time again before my friends
In Toulouse see me, and long also
Before I see Montréal or Puy,
For I'm staying here with en Barral,
Mon Bel Rainier: here's ambience
   And security.
   But Loba!
   Because my eyes
Cannot contain you in their compassing,
They are blurred and wet—my heart
Sighs after you, remembering
   The slender body on you,
   The soft stroke of your voice,
    A smile
   Your face wore once—

Your name is such the best are envious, and
You can afford to let their bitchery run.
Your welcomes are so greatly prized, men come
   Only to hear and see. Beauty's dress
Is your soft speech and youth, your insolent
   Vigor, and your balanced mind.

Na Raimbauda, at Biolh I'm fixing to
Take a garden and a house for hire.
   To be near
   Her I most desire. Among
Such mountains, who can recall the plain?
Lady, lovely lady, how I love you! Life
's nothing without you, death more than life.
May clemency and mercy come upon you,
For my heart's in you, and all my desire.

Lady, when I was within your hall,
It seemed St. Julian must have been my host.

God never made such a perfect day
As you formed of that day with your hand.
In your making He made no mistake;
Such arms were cast only to kill me, sure.
I trust your excellence is too good a thing,
        But even if you killed me,
        It'd be my honor,
        And if I died,
I could only die praising, and rejoicing.

Drogoman, senher, s'agues bon destrier

Lord Expositor, if I had a horse
my enemies would be really up the creek.
Even now they get sick when they hear my name called out
                    like quails
          hearing the cry of a sparrow-hawk.
     They value their lives not a denier
they know I am that savage,
          that fierce.

And when I have my double-hauberk on
                    and gird on
          the sword sir Guy gave me not long since,
the earth shakes, there where I walk,
and no enemy of mine is so presumptious that
          he will not yield immediately
                    the right of way.
They're that afraid to hear my step upon the highroad.

          In boldness, Roland & Oliver are my match,
          in galantry, Berard de Monleydier.
                    And I have found
          such renown in tourney that
                    messengers
          come to me in batches, each
               with a ring of gold
          on a black-and white silk cord
          along with such greetings as rejoice my heart.

All ways I have the semblance of a parfait knight
                    which is true,
and I know of Love all his mastery and all
things that pertain to being lover.
                    I swear,
you've never seen one in chamber more agreeable, nor
               with arms in hand

more sobering and powerful.
Ladies who've never seen me love and fear.

And if I had a horse,
a good corsair,
the king would live serene near Balaguier,
and fall into a soft sleep undisturbed.
For I'd keep the peace in Provence
and Montpellier,
and'd give my vow
that brigands and highwaymen would not despoil
Autaves nor the Crau.

And if the king turn from the sea toward Toulouse,
and the count comes out with his mangy pikemen
who cry all day in Gascon
"ASPE! ORSAU!"
I vaunt that the first blow that falls
shall be my blow.
I'll lay about me so that they'll retreat
at double-time for sure into the town,
and I along with 'em
if they don't let the damned portcullis down . . .

And if I reach those cuckolds and slanderers who
with falsity
put down another's triumph
and strike down joy in open and in secret,
they'll know for real what are the blows I measure!
Their bodies,
were they made of iron or steel,
will not be worth a god-damned peacock's feather!

Vierna, from Montpellier I send my best,
and Rainier, may you love this knight, for which
my joy is increased by you, thanks be to Christ.

Tant ai longamen cercat

Long I looked for what I did not need, then
I unclenched my hand
and there, that sunlight lay on it,
            how I do not know.
It came at my bidding lightly and
lightly I took as I desired
            but now
the granted and given and grown-in-use
I have lost by blundering, misused,
have not gained it
and my friends laugh.

Ah Senyer, dear Castiat,
            I die of this villainy!
for my deadly enemy can
            wound me with beauty.
Yet I hope for such good recompense,
from pain of love sweet deliverance
            and end of guile.
But were it not so great a sin to despair . . .

            But perhaps I speak foolishly
            with my famous excess of levity
            yet may be pardoned for it,
            being so much the fool
            that the whole world can see it,
            how I yield to her caprice
            and venture any emprize
            if she so will.

My love without frontier
still she finds fault!
and knowing well what she does
seeks how to give me hurt.

I find no love in her
nor a loving heart
nor any warm decision or tender gain.
I cry mercy and mercy does not come,
I cry mercy and dare turn nowhere else.

Yet doubt is a major party to it here,
far from my lady where I sing alone.
And until I have passed the Rhône
down toward Lombardy
I will not satisfy my heart
how things stand there.

No man could look on you and not have joy.
Compassion is the tongue within your mouth
and all there is of mercy is your eyes.
Where I place my strongest hope and all my trust
I acknowledge you my lady,
and you, my lord,
and send a heart full of warmth and love.

Vierna, I walk bright in loving you,
lacking only sight of Castiat, my lord.

PEIRE VIDAL

Estat ai gran sazo

For a long time I was bitter,
but now am happier than bird in rain or fish in water,
for my lady has sent me a note to tell me
                    "Act like a man, a lover!"
                    And I never thought to have her
                    return me to hope again.

                    God
                    knows I can't be happy
                    unless I return quickly
                    to that soft cage her beauty
                    has put me in.
                    There it's all softness, warm
                    joy, everything courteous.
                    Take everything I possess
                    plow it under!
                    only to do her pleasure.

So good to look upon the way she's fashioned, her
                    love-shooting eyes, I
                    don't know what I'm doing, or
            where I am, she's got me
seized, won, conquered, taken, tied me down, that I
                    cannot turn
left, right or away my love or eyes. All I
            have to do is see her—I
                    sing, I'm
                    happy with everything.

From the thicket, a flushed bird:
the heart is open to the hunter's arrow.
But a thousand arrows!
and her eyes the bow
and the wound so soft!
Were I next God's throne, lady, and you called

I'd run to you,
willingly rendered and humble,
waiting your mercy and choice.
I live under heavy fear of being
enlaced by a desire for
someone I cannot have. But I
            see roses
            in ice-sheets on the roads,
clear weather
in a sky that's overcast.
Birds sing from the snowdrifts.

But I have a spiteful heart toward one
and wish she'd never lived
since, for a blond count,
she threw me in the road.
            Loba!
I think she is a wolf—
she's been taken by a count and
dropped an emperor whose days
all were spent in spreading praise
of her for all the world to hear.
            Who lies
            does not tell the truth.
A false love's done me in the eye but
I have gained a better lady that way.

God save the illustrious marquis
and his lovely sister,
who with her loyal love has known
how to gently conquer me, and
still more kindly, how to keep me.

I have no walled castle
and my land's not worth two gloves,
            but I am lover.

A per pauc de chantar no·m lais

Near to disgust, close to calling quits with song
seeing youth and courage dead
and honest worth that cannot feed itself, for
all men knock it down and boot it out—
wickedness in power that squats
          on the world's chest
          and stuffs its mouth with lies—
scarcely a country where one's head
          is safe from their traps.

The pope, then, and false doctors of the Church,
Christ Jesus, may they live in his anger!
          selling Rome short:
          such damnfools and liars that
the heretics sing in the streets.
And because these start the lie
it's a hard thing for one to go otherwise, and
I don't look for fights.

Fear out of France and from those
          who used to be straight,
for their king is not honest or sincere
          toward man's honor or God's.
The Holy Sepulcher treated as so much real-estate!
He does business like a damned bourgeois to the
dishonor of these French.

That stink you breathe is a world that stinks to heaven.
The stench was painful yesterday?
          Smell it today!
Since the emperor broke from God's goodness
we have not heard of his power increasing,
          nor his honor,

nor knightly prowess. And now
if the fool leaves Richard to rot in his prison, the
English will have their say.

The kings of Spain
give me a general pain.
They intrigue for war among themselves.
So now they're sending horses
iron greys and bays
to the Moors, out of fear:
whereupon their pride is doubled,
whereupon they are cut to pieces.
And if some peace were made among them,
some law and trust established—
but Christ knows that would give them no pleasure . . .

O, when the rich turn crooked
let no man think I am humbled by them!
I am led by a precious joy that is born in me,
holds me rejoicing.
Her love sharp and certain,
clear coming in pleasure,
arms wide in rejoicing.
You're curious?
Do your asking in Carcassonne.

Never sham
never dissimulation
never counterfeit of speech
(a coin ringing true)
never bamboozling friends with a veil
or the chicanery of rouge,
but her own clear color
rising fresh
as an Easter rose.

She is prime above all other beauty, has
    joined her youth with wisdom.
The most courtly take pleasure in her company,
speak with all praise the quality of her favour.

RAIMON JORDAN, viscount of St. Antonin

(end of 12th C.)

VIDAS

I.

Raimon Jordan was the viscount of Sant Antonin, lord of a rich town which is in Quercy. He was a handsome man, generous, good at arms, and a good man at trobar and courting ladies. He loved the wife of Sir Amiel de Pena d'Alberges, a baron of good repute. And the lady was pretty and young and well-taught, and loved the viscount better than anything in the world, and he her.

It happened that the viscount was at war with his enemies, and being wounded in battle, was carried to Sant Antonin for dead. The news came to his lady that he was dead, and she was so grief-stricken that she entered a patarin [catharist] convent. But the viscount healed of his wound, and when he learned that his lady had entered a convent he had such affliction that, from that time, he made neither vers nor canso.

And here is some of his work.

II.

The viscount of Sant Antonin was from the bishopric of Cahors. He loved a gracious lady who was wife to the lord of Pena d'Alberges, a very rich and very strong castle. The lady was beautiful, worthy, highly-prized and much honored, and he very valiant, learned, good at arms, handsome, and a good troubadour, and was called Raimon Jordan. The lady was called the viscountess of Pena. The love of the two of them was beyond measure, so strongly they felt, one for the other.

And it so happened that the viscount went armed into the territory of his enemies. There was a great battle and, sure enough, the viscount was given a death-wound. His enemies claimed that he was dead, and the news came to his lady that he had been killed. From the sadness and grief she had at the news, she went and entered an order of heretics.

But as God willed it, the viscount improved and healed of his wound. No one wanted to tell him that she had gone and entered herself. When he was well he was brought back to Sant Antonin and there they told him how, because of the great affliction she had had hearing of his death, she had entered herself. When he heard that he lost all comfort and laughter and song and happiness. He hid his plaint, his tears, his sighs and terror, and neither rode nor came nor went among the good people.

And in this way more than a year passed in great bitterness, when ma domna Elis de Montfort, wife of Guillem de Gourdon and daughter of the viscount of Turenne, in whom was beauty and youth, valor and courtesy, sent letters to him praying, with very attractive prayers, that for her love he should grow happy and put off the dolor and sadness that he had put on, saying that she would make him a gift of her heart and her body and her love, as recompense for the evil that had seized hold of him. She begged and cried mercy of him, that he might find it worthwhile to come and see her: but if not, she would come to see him.

When the viscount heard these pleasant favours which this noble and worthy lady addressed to him, there began to come a great softness of love at his heart, and he started to put on gayety, to enjoy himself, and he began to come to the plaza and recover solace among the good people, to dress himself up and take companions, and to regain himself in raiment, arms, and pleasantry.

So he dressed himself well and honorably and went to visit Elis de Montfort. She received him with great pleasure and did him great honor. He was gay and happy at the honors and pleasures she made for him in word and deed, while she was very happy at the goodness, the valor, the sense, knowledge and courtesy that she found in him, and did not repent the favours and loves that she had sent him.

And he knew well how to esteem and be grateful to her, and to suggest delicately that she grant him her love, for he believed truly that it was from a good heart and from love that she had sent him those pleasant favours, and he swore that he carried them inscribed in the close of his heart. She did the situation justice for she took him as her knight, received his homage, and gave herself to him as lady, kissing and embracing, and gave him the ring from her finger by way of signature and surety.

Thus the viscount parted from her very happy and very gay. He took up trobar again and singing and enjoying life, and he made her then this canso which goes:

I incline toward you where I have set my intent.

He made many good cansos, of which one is here written down, as you shall hear.

Lo clar temps vei brunezir

I see the clear weather darken
and small birds bewildered, mute
       huddled in the cold,
with no comfort or rejoicing
when I'm so full of joy. My
heart's sighing for
a lady more
graceful than there ever was before,
more joyous than
when leaves and blossoms were
spread in full flower.

       All my thought's on Love, I
       give my deed in his service.
       It redounds much to my credit
       and I should thank God for it,
       for I've been able to discern
       the best the world has got.
       Any one of you would turn
       gladhearted to be welcomed by
          her
         where my thought
         turns & returns.

I am lover & I'll be hers
as long as I've life at all.
And don't think I'll fall
short before she advances me.
I supplicate toward where she lives,
pray, adore and bend with faithful heart
and turn my eyes often toward that place.
       I love her well.

Damn!
I am

in such distress
to see that place
tower and wall!
at least to reassure my heart
that they still stand,
for messenger I've none but
my own heart in warrant.
And if I comfort myself at all
    it's with the thought
    that she'll not
hear nor understand against me aught,
plea of friend or prayer of parent.

In her is all my relief,
I turn toward no other, no
other welcome in:
and ask nothing in turn
but that she keep faith.
That faith so fixed my courage
    and decided it,
that I have not the power to desire
any other love, whatever be it.

And when I say "my relief" don't
think it's only my pride, for
I so love and desire her that
if I had urgent business with Death,
    the robber,
I would not love God so well, nor
beg him to welcome me into Paradise,
    as I beg her she grant me
space of one whole night to lie beside her.

            But as I tell the truth, may He
            grant that I lie beside her.

RAIMBAUT DE VAQUEIRAS

(b. circa 1155—d. after 1207)

VIDA

Raimbaut de Vaqueiras was the son of a poor knight of Provence, from the castle of Vaqueiras, who was called Peirops since he was taken for mad.

En Raimbaut became a joglar, and stayed for a long time with Guillem des Baux, prince of Orange. He had a good voice and knew how to make coblas and sirventes. The prince of Orange increased Raimbaut's personal possessions and honors, advanced him, and had him meet and associate with the right people.

Then he came to Monferrat, to Monsieur le marquis Boniface, and stayed for a long time in that court, where he flourished at wit and arms and in trobar.

And he fell in love with the sister of the marquis who was called Biatritz, and was married to Enric del Caret. He made many good cansos of her, and called her in his cansos "Bel Cavalier." It was believed that she desired him very much in love.

When the marquis went into Rumania, he took Raimbaut with

him and made him a knight. He gave Raimbaut great land with great income from it in the kingdom of Salonika. And there he died.

[The above version is common to 9 or 10 manuscripts. More or less the same version, with slight variations, is also found in the *Carmina Provincialia, Plut. XLI, codex xliii* of the Laurentiana in Florence. In this manuscript a razo is interpolated. I shall indicate the overlap.]

(((.... to Montferrat, to the marquis Boniface. He stayed for a long time with him, flourished at arms and at trobar, and had great reputation in the court. The marquis, because of the great valor that he found in him, made him a knight and his companion-in-arms and (his equal) in clothing.

Here he became enamoured of the marquis' sister, who was called ma dompna Biatrix and was the wife of Enric del Carret. He made many good cansos for her, and called her the "Bel Cavalier.")))

He called her by that name because of an adventure that happened. En Raimbaut could see ma dompna Biatrix whenever he wanted, even when she was alone in her room, by means of a knothole which no one had noticed. One day the marquis came back from hunting, went into the room, and laid his great sword on one side of the bed, turned and went out. Ma dompna Biatrix remained in the room: she took off her mantle, leaving on only the undergarment, then took the sword and girt it around her like a cavalier. Then she drew it forth in a fury, threw it high, caught it in her hand, and went about the room swinging her arm one place and another with the sword. She returned it to its scabbard, then withdrew it and put it back on the side of the bed.

En Raimbaut saw everything that I have described to you through the knothole. After that, then, he calls her "Bel Cavalier" in his cansos: as he says in the first strophe of this canso which begins:

Never thought I'd see
Love subject me so
until a lady held me
in her power completely;
against her pride I'd put
my pride, ordinarily;
but her youth and beauty,
her fine delightful body,
the good gay conversation
of my Bel Cavalier
makes me isolate and shy:
too, a hard heart bridles
itself toward Love, in
one beloved place wherein
he knows it's better to
love his lady alone,
than humble and over-loving, be
envious of everyone.

(((And it was believed that she wished him well in love. Thus he stayed for a long time with the marquis, and had with him much good fortune. When the marquis went to Rumania, he took en Raimbaut with him.)))

Here he had great sadness because of his love for the lady, who stayed behind with us. And he would have remained behind willingly, but because of the great devotion he had for the marquis and the great honor he had received from him, he did not dare tell him no. So he went with him. But always en Raimbaut strove to be powerful at arms and in war, and worthy of the praise given: so he acquired great honor and great wealth. But for all that, he did not forget his sadness, as he says in the 4th strophe of this canso which begins:

No·m platz iverns ni pascors
Not winter or spring please me

and the cobla which goes:

So what's it worth to me? conquests,
riches?
I thought I was already rich
when I was lover,
and loved.
She nourished me, Englishman.
O Love,
I have not loved one single pleasure,
and I know great courts
and great possessions.
Furthermore, as my powers increase,
I grow more irritable with myself.
My Bel Cavalier has the glory,
my joy's denied, escapes me, is gone.
Comfort's not born from having more:
only the irritability
is greater and stronger.

Raimbaut de Vaqueiras lived thus, as you have heard, and he put
on a better face than his heart gave him.

(((He had great realm, which the marquis gave him in the kingdom of Salonika: and he died there.)))

RAZO

I.

Now you have heard who Raimbaut de Vaqueiras was, how and
through whom he came to honor. But I would like to tell you how,
when the good marquis of Monferrat had made him a knight, en
Raimbaut fell in love with madona Beatritz, the marquis' sister, and
sister of madona Alazais de Salutz.

He loved and desired her greatly, being careful that no other
should know of it. Much he advanced her fame and merit, winning
for her many lovers and many friends among other ladies from

near and far. She did him great honor as she greeted him, still he was dying from desire and fear, for he did not dare ask for her love, nor show any sign that he was in love with her.

But, like a man distrait with love, he told her finally how he loved a noble lady who was young and worthy, that he was very intimate with her, but that he did not dare speak the affection he had for her, nor to show it, nor to ask for some love, he feared so much her great riches and her famed virtue. He asked that for God's sake and mercy's sake, she give him counsel: should he speak his heart and his desire and ask for her love? Or die hiding it in fear and in love?

That excellent lady, madona Beatritz, when she heard what en Raimbaut was saying and knew his loving intention—for beforehand she had noticed that he was dying and languishing, desiring her—pity and love touched her, and she said to him:

"Raimbaut, it is fitting that any true lover, if he love a lady, bring her honor and fear to show the love he has toward her. But rather than that he die, I would counsel him to speak his love to her, the desire that he carries for her, and that he ask to be taken as her *servidor* and her lover. Be quite certain, if the lady be wise and courteous, she'll not keep him dangling in evil and dishonor. If anything, she'll value him better and think him more a man. So I counsel you, that to the lady you love you make known your heart and the desire that you have for her; and you should beg that she retain you as her servidor and her knight. For I saw that madona Alazais admitted Peire Vidal as a suitor; and the countess of Burlatz the same, with Arnaut de Mareuill; and madona Maria (de Ventadorn) granted it to Gaucelm Faidit, and the lady of Marseille (Azalais de Rocamartina again) to Folque de Marseille. So I give you this counsel and guarantee that you, by my word and my surety, may pray her and ask her in love."

En Raimbaut, when he heard the advice she gave him, the surety that she made him, and the guarantee that she promised him, he told her it was she herself whom he loved and about whom he had sought counsel. And Beatritz said that it was good, that he should make a forceful effort to speak well, do well, and be worthy, that she would gladly retain him as her cavalier and servidor, and that he should augment himself. En Raimbaut undertook to do well and speak well with great vigor, and to exalt madona Beatritz as much as he could. And he made then this canso which is written:

Era·m requer sa costum' e son us

Now I require his custom and his use
of Love, for her I desire and sigh for,
when the fairest lady ever tells me
I may love as high as I can low:
the best lady that may be, with
wit that's formed, price and honor met
honest and without harm.
Since she has no competition at love, I
give her my expectation and all my heart.

II.

It happened that the lady went to bed to sleep with him. And the marquis, who loved her so much, found them sleeping and was angered at it. As is known, he did not wish to touch them, but took his mantle and covered their nakedness, and took Raimbaut's cloak and went out.

And when en Raimbaut woke he saw what had happened. He threw the mantle about his shoulders and went directly to the marquis. He went down on one knee before him and claimed mercy of him. The marquis, seeing that en Raimbaut realized what had occurred, recalled the pleasures he had had in diverse places. And he said to him covertly—for Raimbaut's asking pardon had not been heard—that he pardoned him since he had returned his robe, and those who heard it thought he was talking about the mantle and that Raimbaut had taken it. The marquis pardoned him and said that henceforth he should not return the robe. And no more was known about it through those two.

Afterwards it came about that the marquis with his powers passed into Rumania—and with the great help of the Church—the realm of Salonika was conquered. He then made en Raimbaut a knight on account of his great feats. He gave him extensive lands and a large income; and there en Raimbaut died.

Out of the forms his fortune took, he made a canso which he sent to Peire Vidal, which goes:

> *Tant ai ben dig del marques*
> I've said so much good about the marquis.

And here you will find some of his work.

III

Now you have heard of en Raimbaut, who and where he was, and how he was made a knight of the marquis of Monferrat, and how he fell in love with ma dompna Biatrix and lived rejoicing because of her love.

Hear now how, for a time, he had great sorrow. This was because of those false and envious people to whom love and courtship give no pleasure, who spoke certain words to the lady Biatrix and against other ladies, saying things like:

"Though the marquis has knighted him, who, after all, is this Raimbaut de Vaqueiras? And here he goes falling in love with such a high-born lady! You ought to know it does you no honor, neither you nor the marquis." And they spread so much filth in one part and another, as such base people do, that ma dompna Biatrix grew angry with Raimbaut de Vaqueiras. And when he begged her for love and cried mercy of her, she would not listen to his entreaties. Instead, she told him he might go make love to some other lady for all of her, and that she would not hear or listen to anything else about it. This is the despair which Raimbaut had for a short while, as I told you at the beginning of this razo.

On account of it he left off singing and laughing, and anything else that might have given him pleasure. And it was a great shame. All this he had because of the blab of liars, as he says in one strophe of the estampida [a lively dance] which you will hear.

At this time there came to the marquis' court two jongleurs from France who were good fiddlers. One day they fiddled an estampida

which had great success with the marquis, the knights, and the
ladies. En Raimbaut took no delight in anything, so that the marquis noticed it and said:

"Senher Rambautz, now what is this, that you do not sing and be
merry when you hear such a cheerful tune from the viols and see
here such a lovely lady as my sister who has taken you as her servidor and is the worthiest lady in the world?" Raimbaut answered
that he would not perform or do anything. The marquis knew of
the quarrel, and said to his sister:

"Lady Biatrix, for love of me and all these assembled, I wish you
could find it fitting to ask Raimbaut that, for your love and grace's
sake, he cheer up and sing and be happy, as he used to do in our
presence." And ma dompna Biatrix was so courteous and had such
mercy that she begged and comforted him, that he should, for love
of her, grow happy again and make a new song.

At which Raimbaut, for this reason [razo] which you have heard,
made the estampida, and it goes like this:

KALENDA MAYA

May Day, hurrah!
neither leaves of tree
not song of bird   not flower or bee
     are what please me,
     my most gay lady.
Until I've heard   that swift herald be
come here to me   and who'll recite me
some pleasant word,   for love excites me,
     and joy
     and draw me
toward you lady, truly:
     and may he
     fall cruelly,
the jelos 'for I leave thee.

My lovely friend,
may God forfend
that the jealous bastard   laugh at my expense.
His jealous bent's
dearly sold if then
a parting it's fostered   between 2 lovers' sense.
My joy would be mastered   without your dalliance,
the whole world festered,   useless my talents.
Such road
I'd go,
no one would see me ever.
That day
I die
lady, when we sever.

How shall I lose her,
give up, surrender,
lady, if rather   I have never had her?
Being loved or lover
not done by thinking faster.
If he keeps his mouth   close as he has to,
a lover knows rather   to increase his honor.
Only handsome phonies   have made great blather.
For, naked
and taken
you're not, nor I pretend it:
believed in,
desired,
I have you all unaided.

Joy was my share,
now I'm leaving here
away from you in anger   Bel Cavalier.
Though I turn not elsewhere
my body, nor tire
in my desire,   for I want no other:
As for the liars,   I know that this will please them.

Lady, in no manner   satisfy or ease them.
    Such barbs
    I'd feel
as they were steel or dire;
    consider,
    ponder
why a heart suspires.

    Lady, most gracious,
    each one cries and praises
your nobility   which is what pleases.
    He who can forget you
    leads life of little valor.
My unique lady,   why do I adore?
For as most worthy   I have chosen you
as fullest in merit   from the best there are;
    courted
    served better
than Erec did Enida.
    Composed and
    completed,
English, this estampida.

These words were made to the notes of the estampida which the jongleurs played on the viols.

Altas undas que venez suz la mar

High waves that come riding across the sea
that the wind drives in upon this strip of land,
      can you give me news of my lover?
      He went out that way,
      do you see him coming back?
           Aie!
        God of Love!
      Sometimes he gives me joy,
      sometimes sorrow.

You, soft wind, who come from where my
love sleeps and stretches out his length,
      bring me a mouthful of
      his soft breath. I open my
mouth for the great desire I have
           Aie!
        God of Love!
      Sometimes he gives me joy,
      sometimes sorrow.

An ill fate to love a foreign soldier,
all his games and laughter turned to tears.
      Never thought that he
      would take advantage of me.
In love I gave him all he asked of me
           Aie!
        God of Love!
      He brought me joy once,
      and now I've sorrow.

Domna, tant ai vos pregada

SO OFTEN, lady, I have asked you
please to love me, & please, that I be
your devoted slave; for you
are noble, educated, have
each honest virtue firmly; so
your love would please me. Since you are
courteous in your every aspect
so that my body's fixed on you
more than any other Genoese,
what mercy if you returned my love!
I'd think myself better paid at last
than if they gave me the city's keys
and all the coin the Genoese
have ever amassed.

YOU THINK you're being courtly, joglar?
What you think you're asking for?
Wouldn't do it anyway, not if I
saw you were going to be hanged and quartered.
A friend of yours?—Look, I'd prefer
better to cut you up instead.
O, very tough luck, Provensal.
Here are some sweet nothings for you:
you cruddy dope, bald-headed asshole!
Think I'd ever love you? Never!
I've even got a husband better
looking. Clear off, you swine!
I don't know you and I'm better off,
    I like it fine.

MOST INTELLIGENT, noble lady,
thoughtful, excellent & gay, o
let me learn from your good breeding!
For you take perception, joy,
nobleness & youth as guides,

feeling, courtesy & worth,
all the insignia of truth.
For all which I am your faithful
lover, never holding back,
begging mercy, humble, frank.
Loving you is my sole pleasure,
but it overcomes and tortures me.
So may it be your choice and end
that I become your lover
and your friend.

JOGLAR, if I follow your argument
right, you sound like some kind of nut.
Idiot, go to hell. You've got
all the good sense of a cat.
This come-on and your sexy talk
disgust me. What you ask of me
I wouldn't do if you were a son of
kings for generations back.
You think I'm stupid maybe?
You won't get your hands on me. If
you think my loving will keep you warm
you're going to be damned cold this winter.
They're animals, these Provensals,
all Mafiosi.

O LADY, control your savagery,
it doesn't become you and it's wearing.
If it would please you, I undertake
to stand on my request, no jest,
for I love you from a true heart,
and you can cast away all fear since
I am only your liege and slave.
I have thought, am sure, and see,
when I look upon your beauty
fresh as any rose in June, that
the world has none more lovely.

Love, I love, and will love, you.
If I'm betrayed, the sin will be
      upon your part.

JOGLAR, let me finish my speech:
I wouldn't prize your provençal
against one word of genoese.
Try in arabic, german, sard—
you'd be just as hard to understand.
I don't give a damn for you besides.
You want to start a fight with me?
If my husband gets to you, you crud,
your nose'll be sitting next your ear!
O handsome sir, I'll tell you all—
I do not *like* your language, hear?
Buddy, my assurances are clear:
CUT OUT, you rigged up Provensal,
      get out of here!

            LADY, you have made me shy,
            bound me with despair, dismay.
            But may I demonstrate? I pray
            allow me to try you hard and show
            how a Provensal can do it, once
                  he's up and mounted.

JOGLAR, I'll not go with you, that's certain,
since that's all you want of me.
You'll do better, by Saint Martin,
to go hunt up Sir Opetí,
maybe he'll give you a nag to ride,
      you joglar-cretin!

Gaita ben gaiteta del chastel

Castle sentry, see you to your guard,
for she I prize as most lovely, good,
I have at my side till dawn,
which comes. I don't call it. Day
ends my play
      l'alba, oc l'alba

Stay awake my friend & call the hour across;
here I'm rich, having what I want most.
I am dawn's enemy
but the misery of the whole long day
gives me annoy
worse than dawn
      l'alba, oc l'alba

And watch yourself, watcher of the tower,
with your jealous, evil-hearted lord,
more envious than the dawn
of us who here speak softly, and of love,
and only fear
dawn is near
      l'alba, oc l'alba

Lady adieu—longer I must not stay;
no help for it, I must be on my way,
but even worse is dawn!
Oppressive, yet how faint I see it rise.
Damn its eyes!
it *wants* to cheat us
      l'alba, oc l'alba

BERTRAN DE BORN

(b. 1135-40—d. before 1215; period of greatest activity 1180-1194)

I.

Bertran de Born was from the Limousin, viscount of Altafort, and had close to a thousand men. He had brothers and tried to disinherit them as if he were king of England. He was chiefly a maker of good sirventes, and made no cansos except two. The king of Aragon said that the tunes of Giraut de Bornelh made good wives for en Bertran's sirventes. And the one who sang for him, his joglar, was a clever and courteous man called Papiols.

Bertran de Born called the count of Brittany "Rassa" and the king of England "Oc e No" and the young king his son "Marinier". He had this habit of stirring up war among the nobles. He roused father against son of the English royal house, until at length, the young king was killed by a bolt from a crossbow in a castle of de Born's.

Bertran de Born had boasted that he thought himself so valiant

143

that he had no need to use all his wits. When the old king captured him afterwards, he asked him: "Bertrans, will you still need all your senses?" and en Bertrans answered him that he had lost all his senses when the young king died. Then the king wept for his son and forgave Bertran, made him gifts of raiment and gave him lands and honors. He lived for a long time in this world, then joined the Cistercian order. And here you will find some of his sirventes.

II.

Bertran de Born was a nobleman from the bishopric of Périgord, lord of a castle called Altafort. He was unremittingly at war with his neighbors: with the viscount of Périgord (Talairan), with the viscount of Limoges (Aimar), with his younger brother Constantin, and with Richard (Coeur-de-Lion), as long as Richard was count in Poitou. He was a good horseman, fighter, lover, poet, wise and effective at talking, and could deal with evil as well as with good.

When he wanted to, he was always master of king Henry of England and his son. He always intrigued to keep war among them, father, son, brothers, each with the other, the king of France with the king of England, etc. If they had peace or a truce among them, he set to immediately, striving with his sirventes to undo the peace, and to show how each was dishonored by it. He had much good luck and much bad luck from the fact that he stirred enmity among them. And he made many good sirventes, of which great things are here written down, that you may see and hear.

Lo coms m'a mandat e mogut (1181)

The count has moved me by sir Arramon Luc d'Esparro
to make for him such a song as will
slice a thousand bucklers into pieces,
and that doublets, actons, hauberks, helmets
shall be buckled, broke and shattered by it. It

will be a work worth waiting for.
And since his reasons have been told to me, and his
rightness squares my reckoning of it,
I could hardly have said him "No"
besides, it strikes me as entirely fitting that they
curse at me in Gascon—when
I admit that I am captured by them.

At Toulouse
past Montagut,
the count shall plant his gonfalon
in the county meadow near the stone
steps. And when he shall have dressed his
tent, we'll come and set up camp around it,
if we have to sleep there three nights without cover.

And when we're all gathered together, the fight
'll be joined on the flats.
Catalans and Aragonese'll fall, fast and thick.
We'll empty 'em out of their saddles, boys,
            so force-powered and vigorously
            we'll make our points.

            And it can only happen that the
stumps of lances will fly against the
heavens,
            stuffs of samite and cisclaton
            and silken banners ripped to shreds,

ropes
carpets
cloths
hooks
pikes
tents and pavillions strewn
all over hell and gone.

King Alfons
to whom Tarascon is as good as lost,
plus William of Montarberon, plus Roger
viscount of Béziers and Carcassonne,
another viscount's son, Bernard-Aton,
with Peire de Lara of Narbonne,
the count of Foix, Roger-Bernard
and young Bernardo of Comminges,
and Sancho, the king's brother, all
            beaten, conquered.

    Down there they think of armoring up
who, over here, will find some occupation.

I hope these most-high barons will always find
the wherewithal to scratch their irritations.

RAZO

Bertran de Born, as I have said to you in other razos, had a brother who was called Constantin de Born, who was a good knight-at-arms, but not a man to concern himself overmuch with honor and valor. Indeed, he always hated Bertran and loved all those who wished en Bertran ill. Once he seized the castle of Altafort, which belonged to them both in common, and en Bertrans recovered it, likewise by force of arms, and chased him out.

Then Constantin went to the viscount of Limoges and asked that he be upheld against his brother. And he upheld him. King Richard also upheld him against en Bertran. Now Richard was, at that time, warring with Aimar, the viscount of Limoges. But Richard and Aimar turned their war against Bertran, ravaging and burning his fields.

Bertrans had made swear together the viscount of Limoges with the count of Périgord who was called Talairan, from whom Richard had taken the city of Périgord without having put himself in any danger, since Talairan was soft and lazy. Richard had also seized Gourdon from Guilhem de Gourdon, who had promised to swear with the viscount and with Bertran de Born and the other barons of Périgord, the Limousin, and Quercy, all of whom Richard had despoiled; for which reason Bertrans blamed him exceedingly, and for all these reasons (razos), made the sirventes:

Un sirventes cui motz no falh (1182)

I have made a sirventes in which no word is missing
            and it never cost me a garlic.
And I have learned such cunning that if I have
            a brother, say,
or a cousin
or a second-cousin,
I'll split the last egg and the half-denier.
                  But then if he wants my portion
                  I'll run him out of the county!

I hold my wits under lock and key these days,
they've gotten me into such scrapes with both
            Aimar and Richard.
For a long while these two have kept me worried,
            but now
they've got such a scrap going between them that
      if the king doesn't separate them,
      they'll have the profit from it—
      each with a knife in his guts.

Guilhem de Gourdon, you've put a hard
                  clapper in your bell
                  and I must say
you ring it hard, which is crazy.
But God keep me, I am fond of you.
And the two viscounts hold you a fool
                  and laughing-stock
on account of the treaty : yet they long
you were in their brotherhood.

Day long I dispute and contend with myself,
defend and attack and struggle within,
                  while men destroy
my lands and my stratagems
make deserts of my orchards,

mixing
the grain with straw.
There is neither bold enemy nor cowardly foe of mine
who does not assault me.

Day long I re-sole and reshape the barons,
recast and unite them,
thinking to get them into the field.
I'm a fool to bother with 'em—
badly made, the most meager workmanship,
as split as the chain of Saint Leonard—
a man would be mad to concern himself.

Talairan does not leap nor trot
nor stirs him out of his district.
He hurls neither lance nor dart
and lives the life of a Lombard.
He is so stuffed with sloth that,
when alliances break up
he yawns, and stretches himself.

At Périgord, near to the wall,
close enough for a man to throw a mace,
astride Bayart,
I / shall / come / armed.
And if I find fat Poitevins, they
shall see how my steel cuts!
brains mixed with armor, a red mud smearing their heads!

God save you and keep you baron,
and aid you and prosper you.
May it be granted you tell Richard
what the peacock tells the jackdaw.

RAZO

One of the times that Bertran de Born was at war with count Richard, he had the viscount of Ventadour, the viscount of Comborn, the viscount of Segur (who was viscount of Limoges), and the viscount of Turenne swear together with the count of Périgord and the burgesses of those walled towns, and with the lord of Gourdon and the lord of Montfort. So they joined in a compact to defend themselves against Richard who wanted to disinherit them, for indeed they wanted the young king Henry, his brother, with whom he was at war (to be their lord).

Richard had taken certain cart-rents from his brother. Since his father had given them to him, the young king had certain cause on account of this thievery of revenue. In all the lands that belonged to Henry, Richard had not left him one safe shelter from the snow. And by this oath which all of these had taken to carry the war to Richard, Bertran de Born made this sirventes to firm them in it, all those men in the agreement they'd made: also to upbraid the young king that he was not the bravest when it came to battle, reminding him that Richard has stolen his cart-rents and that he'd raised up a strong castle dead-center of the country the old king, their father, had given Henry.

And Bertran de Born praised the lords of Puy-Guillem, Clarans, Grignol, and St. Astier, for they were the four great barons of Périgord: and he praised also himself and Turenne and the Angoulêmes. And he says that if the viscount of Bearn-Gavaudan (who was Gaston de Bearn) and top man in all Gascoigne, and if Vezian of Lomanya and Bernart d'Armangnac the viscount of Tartas would fall in with them, for these men also had no love for Richard, they would have enough to make it. If the lord of Malleon (Raoul de Mauléon, father of en Savaric), the lord of Tonnay, the viscount of Toartz, if all these would agree to help those already in it because of the great injustices Richard had done them, fine. And all these were the great barons of Poitou. And for all these reasons en Bertrans made this sirventes:

Pois Ventadorns e Comborns ab Segur (1183)

Since Ventadorn and Comborn with Segur on one side,
Turenne, Montfort and Gourdon on the other
          have made accord
          with Périgord
          and given their word,
since the bourgeois have
already locked themselves into the towers,
          it's time for a song.
          Time I stepped in
with a helluva sirventes to comfort 'em.
I wouldn't want to have a town, even Toledo,
if I couldn't stay there and keep my head safe.

HAIE! Puy-Guillen and Clarans and Grignol
          and St. Astier; what
domains you have! Yes, and I equally, since
I like to know I've something for myself!
     Look at the counts of Angoulême
          who are no laggards
when it comes to land—and have more certainly
than Milord the Waggoner who's lost his wagon.
He wouldn't know a denier if he saw one. Nor
will he go out fearlessly and get some for himself.
     To live with small land and have honor
     is worth more than to reign dishonored
          over an empire, I say.

If the rich viscount who is the Gascons' boss
and holds down Bearn and Gavaudan,
               if Vezian and Bernard and
               the lords of Dax and Marsan
               will move their cans,
Richard'll have his hands full on that side too.
And though he be valiant enough,
with the big army he'll be raising, it
won't be easy to pull that off,

151

ma, will he be sick
getting it past here and hoisting it
            to our measuring stick!

If Talhaborc and Pons and Lusignan stick,
and Tonnay and Mauléon throw
            their weights in the balance,
            if Sivray had a viscount who
            was not either asleep or sick,
we could find strength there too. Let
the lord of Toartz answer the count's threats
and put in with us and not slack, we'll
back our protest against and squush him
            till he gives back
the rights and revenues he's wrenched from us.

    At Clairvaux
    between Poitiers and l'Isle-Bouchard,
        circled by
    Chinon, Mirabeau, Loudun,
they're building a handsome fortress on the quiet
            not giving a damn, right
            smack in the middle of the plain.
    Now I wouldn't want the young king to hear about it,
but I've a healthy fear he'll see it
all the way from Mateflon, it
            gleams that white on the horizon.

As for Philip: we'll see now if he's his father's son,
or if he'll follow Charlemagne's example. And the proof
will be in what happens, how he acts with Taliaferro
who recognized his suzerainty over Angoulême
and got from Philip confirmation in the fief. So.
            Once a king has given
            his word against a thing,
            and that word is YES,

He hasn't got a stomach if he turns and simpers "No" .

RAZO

Bertran de Born called himself Rassa with count Geoffrey of Brittany, who was brother to the young king and to Richard who was count of Poitou. Richard and Geoffrey had both fallen in love with Bertran de Born's lady, na Maeut de Montaignac, as had King Alfons of Aragon and Raimon, the count of Toulouse: she had refused them all in favor of en Bertran, whom she had taken as confidante and advisor.

And because he wished to gather praises for her, he wanted to show count Geoffrey what sort of lady he had fallen in love with, and he praised her in such a way as to show that he had seen her naked and taken. For he enjoyed letting everyone know that Maeut was his lady, and was one who had refused Poitou, for Richard was lord in Poitou, and Geoffrey who was the count of Brittany, as well as the king of Aragon who was lord of Zaragoza, and count Raimon who was lord of Toulouse, so that he says:

> Rassa, al rics es orgolhosa
> E fai gran sen a lei de tosa,
> Que no vol Peitieus ni Tolosa
> Ni Bretanha ni Saragosa,
> Anz es tan de pretz envejosa
> Qu'als pros paubres es amorosa.

He made his sirventes for this reason which I have told you and to criticize the rich who give no gifts, who offer grudging welcomes, who do not sing, who quarrel when no occasion is given, who, when mercy is asked them, give no pardon, nor reward their servants; and those whose conversation consists solely of talk about flying hawks, and no talk of arms or of love is ever heard in their company.

And he wanted Richard to war against the viscount (Aimar) of Limoges, and the viscount to defend himself bravely. For these reasons, the sirventes was made which goes:

Rassa tan creis e monta e poja

Rassa, I rise,
I prosper, I mount her
who is clean empty of deceit, whose sweet excellence
    insults all other women
        by being so.
For there's no one has one quality so intense
or fine, it can subtract from hers one bit.
    Seeing her beauty convinces,
        wins to her service even those
who to their own detraction . smart under it .
So she has the glory and profit from it, for
thus the most knowing and best maintain her
praise, proclaim her charm and valor forever.
As for integrity,
she would not take, or want, more than a single lover.

Rassa, the lady is sharp and clear,
comely and gay and a young devil:
        auburn hair and white, white
        in her body like a hawthorn blossom!
    Her neck is soft, the tits firm, with a back
    that feels like a rabbit under the hand.
Those who pretend to know me well
or well enough,
can guess with ease,
by the clear fresh color,
by the praise and price, in-
comparable as they are, toward
which part it is I incline—and adore.

And she disdains the rich, Rassa!
which shows good sense in a girl so young.
    She's turned down Poitou and Tolosa
    Brittany and Zaragoza. Furthermore
    it is an enviable virtue that she can

be loving to a poor and valiant man.
Since she's taken me as her advisor, I've
counseled her to hold her love as priceless, to
      give it dear.
And she loves this valorous vavassor better than
      any count or lusty duke who might
      hold her in dishonor.

    The rich man, Rassa, who does not make a gift
or lay a welcome, who does not spend or sing,
who quarrels when no occasion has been given,
who, when mercy's asked him, does not pardon,
and gives no recompense to those who serve him,
he irritates me beyond anything.
Gentlemen falconers! God,
      how they annoy me! out
      hunting with the buzzards they own,
      gabbing interminably of flying hawks with
      never a word of love or arms
spoken among the lot!

This I ask you, Rassa, don't
be offended: that plutocrat
who leaves us to our wars, yet never leaves
      off menacing with threats until
      a man who does not want to harm him
      has to restrain himself, even so, is
this ugly state not worth more than falconry? and
      these eternal hunting parties, that
      no solid courage would embrace or welcome?
(Mauris, with en Agar, his lord,
conducted war with a proper valor.)

The viscount here is hot to defend his honor :
the count demands the garlic now by Christmas.
They'll see each other out then around Easter.

Mariniers, you have the honors, while
we down here have a changed lord and a
good fighter—as a tourney rider.
And I beg of Golfus de Lastors
that he not let my songs upset him too much.

Papiols, I'm sending you on the run again,
back to the court of my wicked Bel-Senhor.

RAZO

Bertran de Born was the lover of madomna Maeut de Montanhac, the wife of Talairan (brother of the Talairan who was count of
Périgord), who was such a lady as I have described to you in the
razo to the sirventes of the "borrowed lady." And, as I have told
you, she broke up with and dismissed him over the matter of Guischarda, the wife of the viscount of Comborn, who was a worthy
lady from Bourgogne and sister of en Guishcart de Beaujeau. She
was a lovely lady and well-educated, accomplished with all her
beauty.

En Bertrans had already praised her highly, recounting and singing of her even before he had seen her. He was her friend because of
the good reports he had had of her, and before she had come to be
married to the viscount of Comborn. And because her arrival made
him happy, he made these coblas (couplets) which go:

> Limousin, open, courteous land, oh
> I know what honors will increase you soon,
> for joy and valor, pleasure, gaiety,
> solace, love's service too and courtesy
> are dealt you now. First of all there's body;
> ladies with lovers had better tie them down.
> A woman should be, as this one is, built.
>
> Recompense and gifts, dress and largesse
> nourish love as water does a fish;
> so valor and good manners, arms, prowess,
> tourney-grounds decked out, and courts and wars.
> Those with courage, and those who pretend it,
> had better show it now, and no pretense,
> for they have sent Guischarda here to us.

So because of the lady Guischarda, madomna Maeut grew very
cool with en Bertran, for she believed that he preferred Guischarda
to her and that she (Guischarda) had been making love with him.
Because of this separation, he made the *domna soisseubuda* and the
sirventes which goes:

Eu m'escondich, domna

Lady
I clear myself toward you,
guiltless
of what they have said to you of me.
            And I pray you mercy
            that no man may mess
with
or confuse your fine body, loyal,
            without artifice,
frank, humble, commanding and full
            of pleasure toward me, lady,
and by recounting lies put quarrel between us.

I hope I lose my sparrowhawk at first cast,
may lanners come and kill her on my fist
carry her off picked,
            may I see her plucked
if I do not love you firm and with more longing
than desire I have for any other, even if
            she accord me her love
            and keep me in bed.

To make the exculpation to you stronger, I'll
call the worst luck down upon myself:
if ever, even in thought, I've failed you,
when I shall be in bedroom or in orchard
            alone with a woman, may I be put
            out of commission in such a way that
I cannot raise the necessary capital.

When I sit down at a gambling board
I hope I never win a denier.
May I never set my marker on a good play
and may I throw snake-eyes forever,

if I've ever even asked another lady
other than you
whom I desire, and prize, and love.

May I my own castle be part-owner of—
   Let there be four inheritors
         dividing the tower,
without any of us ever being able to agree.
Rather, I wish myself the dire necessity of
a crossbowman
a doctor at all times
mercenaries
a bodyguard
and someone to watch the gate besides,
        if ever I had the heart
        to love another woman.

May you quit me for another lover and I
never know to whom to turn for help:
let the wind drop when I put out to sea, let
porters beat me up and kick my butt
in the king's court itself,
the dead-center of.
Let me be the first to flee when the battle locks and clashes,
       if he told you the truth, the one
       who fed you this balderdash.

      By damn!

With my buckler on my back and my hood on crooked,
let me ride in bad weather on a horse a bitch to handle
with the reins too short and the damned stirrups dragging,
long stirrups on a short horse that likes to trot in mud,
to an inn that will be cold, and where my very entrance
will irritate the innkeeper : if he didn't lie,
       the SOB who handed you this rubbish!

Say I have a fine duck hawk,
lively, newly-moulted, trained
steady on the take and
                    ready to the hand,
one who can overtake
                    any bird,
                              swans as well as cranes,
                              herons white or black,
will I then want another?
a badly-moulted chicken-hunter?
                    fidgety and fat
                    who cannot even fly?
Lady, is it reasonable?

                    As for you envious liars
                    and sneaky slanderers,
                    now you've got me out of
                    favor with my lady,
            I'd be damned glad if you left me to myself.

Greu m'es descendre charcol

Depressing to dismount the siege-machines
          and you know?
I do not think it pretty that
I've not seen a fight, not even an ambush
         in almost a year?
And I sit here very depressed
because they stay out of it for fear,
the rest of us staying likewise . out
of love for the lord of Molierna.

        But that lord
         who has Bordeaux,
how he points them up and grinds them down!
        tests them like
        the edge of the knife!
But they are too thick and sluggish, even—words,
posting a notice can cut them.
        Holier than priors,
thanks to the grinding stone, they'll all
get to heaven.

        Not even Berlais de Mosterol
        nor en Guilhems de Monmaurel
        had so hot a heart as our barons this
        year at the beginning of summer.
Now that the cold comes down, daring
turns to cowardice
        when the clear weather darkens.

As for the lord of Mirandol
        who holds
        Croissa and Martel,
I don't believe he'll rise this year
until he sees what the French are doing
        who ride toward home

turning to utter threats . I'm
not taking bets
but they don't believe their own boasting, sure
they'd rather sit it out till Easter
for here in the Limousin we've only
rain, and winter weather settling.

But then,
count Richard would rather steal
Benaujes here
near to Bordeaux
than Cognac or Mirabeau or Chartres,
                or St.-Jean.
He'll take, only with difficulty, Botenan,
but will not, for fear of his lord,
                wet his breeches
            for which I think
        Merlin might mock him.

Urgelians, Catalans, Aragonese,
you should moo your grief,
for you have as lord and chief
                only a great cow,
who praises himself in his singing and takes
more deniers than honor . Besides, he
                hung his predecessor
so he's damned himself into the bargain .

        I turn toward where the tooth hurts me,
                toward her where it seems right that I
reproach and call her from deceit and treason.
For because of her capricious desires, I
suffer, that these false hypocrites feign love
            for her whom honor governs.

I know a tiercelet, moulted,
never took a bird : but

frank, courteous, agile, with whom
I've exchanged the name of Tristan.
And worth all that this seems, she's
taken me as lover, so has given me greater
        riches than
if I were king in Palermo.

        Tristan, for your love, they who
        mock me will have the pleasure of
        meeting me in the tourney-lists
        in Poitou.

Since the Queen of Love
has taken me as lover, it may be
that I may make a five
        and she win three.

RAZO

In whatever way he could, Bertran de Born was always riling king Philip of France with his sirventes and coblas, reminding him of his past errors and defeats. He would tell Philip that, whatever his words or deeds to the contrary, the king of France was hardly eager to meet Richard on the field of battle. But when he saw Philip's feeble-heartedness, king Richard leapt to war, and robbed and burned, and seized castles, market-towns, and cities, killing and taking prisoners. The barons, to whom peace was uncongenial, were very cheerful at seeing this, and Bertran de Born more than any, for he loved war better than other men, and he believed that it had been on his say-so that Richard had started the war. For he and Richard called themselves Oc-e-No, as you will hear in the sirventes he made as soon as he heard that Richard had rushed into the campaign, the one that begins:

No puosc mudar un chantar non esparga

Since Oc-e-No has set the fire and drawn blood
I can't help it, I've got to sing and send it.

Now a good war makes a niggardly lord
turn lavish and shell out handsomely.
        So naturally
        it pleases me
to see the war-set pomp of the two kings, for they'll
   need stakes, pikes, ball and bowstrings,
      the tents rising, the sleeping outside, we'll
         find them by the hundreds, the thousands! Long
         after us the exploits shall be sung. I,

haven't I taken blows upon my shield,
        and dyed red
      the white of my gonfalon?
yet to do this I have to suffer and pinch my purse,
for Oc-e-No plays with loaded dice.
I'm not lord of Rancon or Lusignan
   and even worse,
can hardly war beyond my own fields
     without some moneys to back me;
but can bring my know-how and a good strong arm
with a buckler on my neck and a basin on my head!

If Philip hadn't burned his boat
   before Gisors, or drained the tank,
      if at Rouen he'd entered the park by force;
      if he'd laid the siege from both the heights
        and the narrow valley, then
no one'd got a brief through without pigeons.
But I know now he'd like to equal Charles
who surely was the best of his forebears
—took Saxony and Apulia as well.

It was shame got Richard into it
and with honor he worked it out:
he fought with one that no man had found frank.
  So I don't think
    he'll give up Cajarc and Cahors,
      old Oc-e-No!
No, he knows when he's got a *tour de force*.
          A heart for war?
          That he's got, and if
the old king gives him the treasure of Chinon,
he'll have both the power and the bait.
As it is, his pleasant expenditures and difficulties
          are so great
that his enemies—and his friends—are sunk.

Ship still on sea, the lifeboat shot, no running lights,
tacking close to the reefs in nasty weather.
If my heart were stronger than arrow from a bow, still
the boat's pitching, and I never caught a fish.
          And I tell you, count,
I perform for her who does not wish to keep me,
who backs me on no day, promise or limit.
  Those joys?
    and flowered?
      already withered with blight. But

      go, Papiols, run, and quickly,
        be at Treignac before fiesta.
Tell Roger and all his family that I
can find no more rhymes in *omba, om* and *esta*.

Mei sirventes volh far dels reis amdos (1194?)

I want to make half-a-sirventes upon two kings,
    and we shall see which of the two is more a knight!
        Alfons, the valiant king of Castile, who is en route
            and will want soldiers,
            or Richard
who spends gold and silver by the gallon and hogshead
and makes all his pleasure in spending and giving,
            refusing all truce,
and seeks war with more heat than a sparrowhawk cast at a quail!

If both kings are intrepid and bold, without fail
            we'll see soon
            fields strewn
    with wreckage and quartered corpses, with
        saddle-trees and brackmarts,
            helms and escutcheons,
everywhere corpses split through like kindling
        from the head to the fly,
            and destriers on every side
            running at random,
                and many long lances stuck through
                    broadsides and chests,
witnesses
of great joy and tears, great distress and wild glee,
great will the hurt be, but the gain greater!

Horns, drums, standards, pennons and oriflammes, horses
black and white
that's what we'll see soon!
And it'll be good living then
liberating what the usurer owns.
By God, there won't be one safe packhorse on the roads,
        we'll make the bourgeois shiver!
Merchants won't get away anymore, walking the roads in peace,

the damned costermongers, the route to France at least,
and every man is rich who'll just up and plunder.

And if I see the king, I have faith in God I'll
either come off living, or by the sword and lance,
I'll come off in quarters!

And if I come off living, it'll mean great riches,
and if I die—a great deliverance.

Be·m platz lo gais temps de pascor

SPRING IS A JUICE, a rejoicing, forcing
leaves out, flowers up.
I like the noise of birds who make
their singing ring in the woods,
and see tents
on the meadows raised,
and pavillions raised,
and a very hellish delight to see
armored horses and armed knights ranging
down the field.

And on the roads I have delight to see
the rabble with their goods in flight
pressed by the skirmishers, and behind
outriders,
        the army crowding in.
And it pleases me in my heart to see
strong castles at siege,
ramparts broke and riven, and
an army on the fosse-brink gudgeoned
        in
between palisade and ditch
the stakes close-set.

And I love beyond all pleasure that
lord who horsed, armed and beyond fear is
forehead and spearhead in the attack, and there
emboldens his men with exploits. When
        stour proches and comes to quarters
        may each man pay his quit-rent firmly,
        follow his lord with joy, willingly,
for no man's proved his worth a stiver until
many the blows
he's taken and given.

Maces smashing painted helms,
glaive-strokes descending, bucklers riven,
this to be seen at stour's starting!
And many valorous vassals pierced and piercing
    striking together!
And nickering, wandering lost through the
    battle's thick,
brast-out blood on the broken harness,
    horses of dead men and wounded.

And having once sallied into the stour
no boy with a brassard may think of aught, but
the swapping of heads and hacking off arms—
for here a man is worth more dead
    than shott-free and caught!

I tell you,
I have no such savour of eating soft
food and sleeping and tasting hot wines
as hearing the cries from each side coming
    "AT THEM! "
and see
waiting under the trees
horses whicker and strain,
to hear the shout
    " a RESCUE! to AID! "
and see fall in the fosse and on the green earth
the mighty and mean, and
see in the flanks of the fallen
    the broken
butt-end of lances, their banners flaming!

    Pawn your castles, lords,
    pawn your towns and cities!
    Before you're beat to the draw
        unsheath those swords!

Papiols, rejoice and go
with all haste to Oc-e-No
and tell him that we've got too much
damned PEACE down here!

THE MONK OF MONTAUDON

(c. 1180—1215)

VIDA

The Monk of Montaudon was from the Auvergne, from a castle that had the name Vic, which is near Orlac. He was a nobleman who had turned monk at the abbey of Orlac, and the abbot gave him the priory of Montaudon. There he behaved himself and worked for the good of the house. While still in the monastery, he made coblas and sirventes from arguments that were current in the neighborhood.

Knights and barons took him from the monastery, giving him anything that pleased him or that he wanted, anything he asked them for: and he carried it all back to his priory in Montaudon.

He enriched his own church and caused it to flourish, always wearing his monk's robes. He turned then to Orlac, pointing out to the abbot the improvements he'd made for the priory in Montaudon, and asked to be given the privilege of conducting himself under the direction and judgment of King Amfos of Aragon: and the abbot granted it to him.

The king recommended that he eat meat, court the ladies, and sing and compose songs: and he did so. He was made lord of the court of Puig Ste.-Marie, and given the privilege of awarding the sparrowhawk. For a long time he had lordship in the court of Puig, until that court was in decline.

Then he left there and went down into Spain. All the kings, barons, and valiant men of Spain paid him great honor and held great fiestas for him. He entered a priory in Spain called Villafranca which belongs to the abbey of Orlac. When the abbot gave it to him, he enriched it, and made it flourish and prosper. It was in that place his life ended, and he died.

L'autrier fuy en paradis

I WAS IN PARADISE the other day
so you see me still happy and
gay from the welcome given me
by God, whom all things obey,
earth, valleys, mountains, sea.
He said, "Monk, why is it I see
you here and not in Montaudon
where you have better company
    than I have here?"

"Lord," I said, "it's a year or two
I've been cloistered up, and now
I've somehow lost the favour of
the barons: for love of You
I've grown a stranger to their love.
And only Randos, the one in Paris,
has not mistaken or deceived me,
or complained of the rarity
    of my visits."

        "Monk," He said, "I'm unhappy to see
        you fettered up in a monastery,
        not fighting or even making tensos,
        not in any neighbors' riot—
        you yawn and are so blessed quiet—
        I like the song and laughing better,
        the world's more lively for the gaff
            and Montaudon gets a rake-off."

        "Lord, I'm afraid I sin, writing these
        coblas and cansos. Always saying
        the opposite of what one knows
        one could lose your love and You,
        so I leave the bargaining and gain.
        The century does not ease me. So

173

I'll go back, sing matins, and give
up my trip to Spain."

"You're wrong, Monk, why you should run
to that king who has Oléron.
Has he ever shown you ill favour? So.
He was right to let you go.
Think of how many marks sterling
he's willing to lose against your pair
to get you out of a corner!"

"Lord, I'd be glad to see him though
I wouldn't go against your will.
Why'd You let him be put in prison?
Now the Saracen fleet under full
sail makes headway—you ignore it—
and if it makes rendezvous in Acre
the Turks will make short work of that!
Anyone would have to be an idiot
to follow You into battle."

Molt mi platz deportz e gaieza

I like gayety and horsing around, good
food, fine gifts, good tilting fields:
I like a comely and courteous woman,
one who's not too embarrassed to answer.
And I like a rich and generous man
who keeps his malice for his enemies.

I like a man who calls me affably
and unfastens his purse without having
to be asked first, and a rich man who
doesn't feel he has to put me down;
I like someone who speaks nicely to me
and doesn't have to get into an argument;
like to fall asleep when it's thundering hard
and to eat a fat salmon in mid-afternoon.

And it relaxes me in summer to
stretch out by a brook or fountain when
the meadows are green and the flowers new
and the birds all chirm and twitter: and then
if my girl finds out where I'm holing up
I turn her over and have a quick one.

Bless them who give me a hearty welcome
and don't go scrummaging for excuses.
I enjoy the time I spend with my girl
necking, and more if she wants to make it.
Like to see my enemy lose a good thing
and better if it's me who took it off him.

And good companions please me fine
when I'm surrounded by enemies and
I hear someone else speak my piece—
and the buggers listening without budging.

L'autre jorn m'en pugiey a·l cel

I ascended to heaven again last week,
it was to St. Michael I went to speak
    as I was bid,
and I overheard a fine complaint.
    Hear how it went.

St. Julian came before God's shoe
and said: —Lord I complain to you
    as a man offended.
For I've been stripped of all my due
    and badly treated.

Whoever wanted lodging used to
ask me about it in the morning,
    that was my job.
Now I can't give the advice away,
    even to sinners.

They've taken all my powers from me,
they don't pray to me night or morning.
    Even those with a bed
leave in the morning to move below.
    I've been dishonored!

From Carcassonne or from Albi,
much less Toulouse, do they implore me
    as they were used.
But in Catalunya I've all my rents
    for there I'm loved.

In the Limousin and Périgord
the count and king kill more of them,
    I'm loved besides.
They have some down in Quercy, but there
    I'm satisfied.

From the Rouergue to Gavaudan, I
don't brag or complain of how things stand
    but there are enough
of those who still, each one, give me
    goodwill and no guff.

Without welcome, in the Auvergne
you can find an inn for the night,
    no reservation.
They may not know how to talk polite
but find the conversation pleasant.

Throughout Provence and among the barons
I asked for further informations.
My name was not invoked nor raised
by the Provensals. Nor by the Gascons
    was much praised.

Fort m'enoia, so auzes dir

So you'll know it—what annoys me most, and right
it should, is that blowhard who's always going
        "to do something" for me.
I hate a braggart who's going beat
        the world—and a horse
that pretends to be lame, more of the same.
And so help me, what gives me a pain in the neck
is that young man who carries, everywhere,
        a buckler, and's never taken a stroke.
A pox on chaplains, on monks who wear beards,
and the flatterer with his well-filed beak.

I detest a woman who's "poor and proud"
—or a man who loves his wife too much
even if she's a lady from Toulouse,
        and while I'm bitching,
I put down that sort of knight who lords it
        far his own region,
who at home they entrust with the egregious duty
        of grinding pepper, or
watching casseroles in the kitchen.

            I hate, prodigiously, a coward
            who always carries around a banner.
            And what gives me an honest pain in the tit
            is mediocre hawks on a good hunt, or
            an enormous pot with a bit of meat in it.
            And by the good St. Martin, I hate
            a little wine cut with a lot of water!
            Another impossible irritation is
            to meet a blind man in the morning,
            or a cripple either. I just can't stand
            their company on the road all day long.

What gives me a rash is waiting too long
at table, for the instruments to finish.
And another thing that rubs me wrong is
      tough meat that's badly prepared,
or a priest who's both a perjurer and liar.
Or an old whore who's too tough down there.
And by Saint Dalmat, I dislike the expression
   on the face of a wretch
      who's getting too much
         consolation. I hate
to travel when there's ice on the road,
and another thing that's a pain in the ass
is to have to ride, wearing the full load of
armor, at gallop. And people who curse at dice.

      And by the eternal life, it grates me
      to eat in dead winter without a fire,
      or to sleep with an old fart of a woman
      who lets fly
         on my thigh a
      low ructation from the tavern.
      At night, it gives me great distress
         to have to call the varlet
         to come and rinse the pot out
      again.
      And it breaks my heart altogether to see
      a grim husband with a lovely wife and he
      prevents her from according, or even
         offering me anything.

And it irritates me, I swear by Saint Salvat,
to hear a vile violinist in a good court.
And I tell you truly that it hurts my can
to see too many brothers on a small piece of land:
and—at gambling—to have a partenaire who,

after I've thrown the most impossible of plays,
    has only laid down a denier.

And by Saint Marcel, I'd rather freeze than see
two skins on a single coat that's given me.
In a rich lord's hall, I hate meager cheer, and
one castle with too many inheritors.
And at tourney—o hell,
the javelins and quarrel-bolts bore me to tears.

May God aid me soon, I find it trying to sit
at a long table with a short tablecover. And it
makes me itchy when they put to cut the roast
a big, red lackey with his hands all scabs, and
I hate a heavy hauberk where the mail don't fit.

And Christ! it annoys me to stand at the door
when the weather's bad and it's raining hard.
Mmm, something else I can't put up with long,
that's to watch a squabble between good friends,
and still more annoying to realize that they
    —both of them—are in the wrong.

A couple other things I don't care a rap for:
to ride along without a cape in a downpour—
or to find a pig tied near my horse, that
eats up everything in the horse's trough.
And why have a saddle where the saddle-tree's loose?
God, I can't stand to have a buckle or a clasp
that doesn't have a tongue. And I dislike a man
who's clumsy, awkward, and maladroit at home.

    Another item that's painful to bear
    and that's an ancient pro who's too prettied up
    or any poor strumpet giving herself airs.

I hate ladies who're too proud of their legs.
And I hate down to the dregs, *saalve regina*,
a big fat woman with a tight vagina.

You know, he strikes me as unbearably cheap,
a lord who squeezes his underlings too hard. But,
the thing I hate most in the world is being
        —sleepy—
and unable to fall asleep.

THE MONK OF MONTAUDON

Autra vetz fuy a parlamen

By good luck a few days back,
I was at a conference in heaven again.
Saints' statues were griping: would've moved a stone,
about ladies who use rouge and cream.
I heard them complain to God of those
who force cosmetics up in price
painting their faces until they gleam,
and who should leave well-enough alone.

But God spoke to me very frankly:
"I've been listening so much, Monk,
my eardrums ache. I give it up
and grant the saintly statues their rights.
Will you go down for love of Me
and dammit, make the ladies quit?
I can't stand this racket anymore!
And if they won't swear off the paint
I'll descend and wipe them out entire!"

—Lord, God, I pleaded, you should have
        pity and measure
    on ladies whose nature
's to guard their faces like a treasure;
and you ought not to get so upset.
The statues will not have told you that,
for they'll never permit, from jealousy,
the ladies ahead of them, seems to me.

"Monk," said God, "your argument is
deceiving, false, and sinful too.
My creature beautifies herself
without my express command. So,
they'd be my equals, would they?
I make them age a bit each day:

not with cosmetics or burnishing then,
can they turn their faces young again."

—Lord, you speak with too much arrogance
from your lordly pride and highness.
Soon there won't be left a drop of
makeup on earth, if you don't
come to some agreement with them.
Either make all beauty last
in ladies up to death, or else
make all the cosmetic disappear
so that nowhere can anyone find an ounce.

"Using such false arguments, Monk,
you fall to excess. Surely it
does not befit a lady to
improve her natural face with goo.
Even if you lower yourself to praise it,
they themselves should not permit
such beauty. You know, I think I see
a cure: I'll close up the skin
between their legs so they can't pee."

—Lord, who's well-madeup goes well,
so they take care of themselves and make
the fortification hard and thick
with pee, so it won't easily flake
off. Even though you don't want them
to make improvements, if they do,
please Lord, don't close up that skin:
foremost be grateful they make themselves
lovely, and save you all that work.

"Monk, for wearing rouge and powder
I'll see they get many a stroke down there,
and don't think your pleading will get them off.
Man has to make them bend low and stay there."

—Then hell may burn them, Lord, for I
can't plaster up their holes for them;
for when I come to a river bank, why
I just have to get in and swim.

"Monk, it's too much to let them off,
this pissing can ruin the fard supply.
No. I shall send them such punishment
that not one shall ever pee again."

—One, Elis de Montfort, Lord, forgive her
and make her pee, for she has never
had to or wanted to use the stuff,
and's had no complaint, from saint or lover.

Pois Peire d'Alvernhe a chantat

Since Peter of Auvergne once sang
of troubadours now past and gone,
I'll sing now from my wise and fit-
ful knowledge of those who profess to play
    at trobar today.
I hardly think they can get sore if I
score their performances a bit . . .

    The first is from Sant Disdier,
    Guillem, who sings too readily.
    And there are handsome words he's sung,
    but he doesn't want a serious love
    so acquires no fine mastery, and
    always gets a miserable welcome.

    The second's of Sant Antonin
    the viscount—'s never enjoyed love.
    He always makes a lousy opening
    because his first love was a tease.
    He's never wanted one since then, though
    night and day his eyes are running.
        Must be a disease.

And the third one is from Carcassonne,
Miravals with his courtly words and sounds.
He's often given his castle away: in
a whole year, not a month hardly
or a kalends passes, it is not taken
from him, for there's hardly danger
that he'll manage to take it back again.

    The fourth, Peirols, an Auvergnat,
    30 years he's worn the same old suit,
    it's better seasoned than kindling wood;
    and if anything, his songs have worsened.

185

At Clermont he spends all his time
with whores, so makes no worthy song.

And the fifth is Gaucelm Faidit
who's a lover turned insane
(i.e., a husband) and married her
who was only his follower.
Now we hear neither vows nor cries,
even his cansos no longer bray
the whole way from Uzerche to Agen.

And then the sixth, Guillem Azemar—
there never HAS been a worse joglar;
many an old suit he's had to take.
And he sends his songs to such a place
as cannot match his thirty years.
Saw him recently, poor and out of sorts.

Arnaut Daniel, that's seven, and
he's never in his life sung well—
some mad words no one can understand.
But since he set the ox to hunting
the hare, since he put his chest
against the current, his songs
have not been worth the breath you need
    to sing 'em.

En Tremolet, the catalan who
makes his tunes so easy and plain
    and his songs too, but
    he's nothing: combs
his hair on top as if he had some.
Thirty years he's wanted to make albas
and's made nothing but the grimiest smut.

And the ninth, Arnaut of Marvelay:
I always see him in a bad way for

his lady shows him no clemency,
treats him badly, will not have him around.
His eyes are always crying for mercy and
that moisture speaks louder than his song.

    Sail de Scola is the tenth, a
    joglar who has turned bourgeois
    in Brajairac where he buys and sells:
    and when he's sold his harness as well,
    well then, he goes off to Narbonne
    with a false song asking for recompense.

The eleventh is Giradon lo Ros
whose livelihood is others' cansos,
and is dull and tedious to everyone.
Moreso since he thought himself so honored
for holding a tenso with Anfos' son
where neither was saying nuthin really.

The twelfth is en Folque, that bore
from Marseille, a merchant, nothing more.
And that was a foolish oath he took
when he swore he'd make no more cansos.
I lie pretty well at my own discretion,
but he's belied his whole profession.

A 13th there is, and is a neighbor,
Guilhem the marquis—he's my cousin
so I can't say what I'd like to, fully.
But, with his scant songs, a dozen,
the poor little shrimp can't earn a penny,
and he's old, with a moustache and a beard.

    Peire Vidal's down here toward the end
    and he isn't altogether there.
    He turns his work with a silver tongue
    but vulgarly: he was a furrier once.

Since he made himself a cavalier
he's lost both memory and his sense.

Guillem de Ribas, the fifteenth, to
look in his face you have to look down.
He sings willingly if not well
and dogs you up and down the halls.
I never have seen him outfitted well.
He lives rather poorly and without fame.

And the 16th too, will never have fame,
that false-hearted monk of Montaudon,
who tensos and fights with everyone.
For Dionysus he gave up God
and whatever canso or vers he's made
men shall heave them to the wind.

This vers the Monk has made and first
spoke it out forthright at Caussada,
and sent it down past Lobeat
as a present for en Bernat.

GUILHEM DE CABESTANH

(c. 1190—1212)

VIDA

Guilhem de Cabestanh was a knight from the country of Rossillon, which borders on Catalonia and Narbonne. He was very handsome as well as distinguished in arms and in chivalry.

There lived in his country a lady named Seremonda, the wife of Sir Raimon of Castle Rossillon, a rich nobleman that was harsh, evil, fierce, and haughty. And Guilhem de Cabestanh fell in love with the lady and made cansos and sang them for her. And the lady, who was young and noble, beautiful and kind, loved him more than anything in the world. And Raimon of Castle Rossillon was told; and he, angry and jealous, looked into the thing, and saw that it was true, and set a close watch on his wife.

And there came a day when Raimon of Castle Rossillon found Guilhem alone in the country and killed him; and he took the heart out of the body and had a squire carry it to his home; and he had it roasted with pepper and served to his wife. And when the lady had eaten the heart of en Guilhem, Raimon told her what it was. When she heard that, she fainted away. And when she came to she said, "My lord, you have given me such a good meal I shall never take another." Hearing her speak thus, he came at her with his sword and would have split her head, but she ran to a balcony and threw herself down to her death.

Lo dous cossire que'm don' amors soven

The sweet softness with which love serves me often
Makes me write much vers of you, my lady.
I gaze imagining on your bright body,
Desiring it more than I can let you know.
Although I seem to swerve and stand aside
It is for your sake, not to deny one whit
That I supple and bend toward you in all love's ways.
Too often, lady, I forget, and so
Implore mercy and am forced to praise
When beauty finds itself mere ornament.

May the love you deny me hate me always
If my heart ever turns to love another.
Yet you've left me sadness, taken all my laughter,
Stiffer suffering than I, no man can say
He's felt, for, you, whom I most want
Of anything on earth, I have to
Disavow, deny, pretend
I've fallen out of love, and all
For fear,
Which you must take wholly on good faith,
Even those days when I do not see you.

Your face and smile I keep in memory's place,
Your valor, your body smooth and white.
If my Faith were as faithful as that image there,
I'd walk living into Paradise.
I am rendered so utterly
Yours, without reservation,
That not one who wears ribbon
Could bring me any joy,
Nor I prize the compensation
Even if she made me lover
And had me sleeping with her,
Taken against your simple straightest greeting.

The charm of how you are gives me such joy
That my desire pleasures me every day.
Now totally and in full you mistress me,
How overmastered I am, I can scarce say,
But even before I saw you
I'd determine to serve and love you.
And so I have remained,
Alone and without aid
At your side: and lost by
Doing so many gifts.
Let who desires them have them.
I'd rather wait for you, even
With no understanding between us,
For my joy can come from you alone.

May mercy and love descend upon you, lady,
Before the sickness inflames,
May joy burn us, tears and sighs banished,
May neither rank nor riches separate us.
All good's forgot
If I do not obtain
Some mercy, beautiful thing.
It would give some relief at least
If you answered what I've asked.
Either love me, or not at all, for now
I don't know how it is.

Because I find no defense against your valor,
May you have pity, so it end in honor.
May God never hear prayer of mine if I
Would take the rents of the four richest kings there are,
Put together,
Against the chance of finding mercy with you.
For I cannot
Stir one jot
Away from you where my love is set.
And if you found you could

Accept it
With a kiss
I'd never want to be dissolved from this.

Frank and courteous lady,
Come hell or high water,
Anything that pleased you
No matter how forbid,
I would set me to it.

Ray, the good and beauty
Residing in my fair lady
Has enlaced me softly
Taken me completely.
How can I deny it?

GAUCELM FAIDIT

(1185—1215)

VIDA

Gaucelm Faidit was from a town called Uzerche in the bishopric of Limousin. He was the son of a bourgeois, and sang as badly as it is possible for any man to sing in this world. And he made many good tunes with good words. On one occasion, when he'd lost all his money in a dice game, he turned jongleur.

The man was prodigious in size, and ate & drank so much that he grew fat beyond measure. And he had a pain in his backside for a long time, looking to seize honor, for, for more than 20 years he went on foot through the world, before either he or his cansos were accepted or wanted.

And he took as wife a professional, whom he led for a long time with him through the courts, who was called Guillelma the Nun. She was very pretty and well-taught, and grew to be as big and fat as he was. She was from a rich town called Alest, in the March of Proensa, which was under the lordship of Bernart of Andussa. Then the marquis Boniface of Montferrat settled money and equipment and clothing on him, creating great prestige for him and for his songs. And now you will hear an alba of his which goes:

GAUCELM FAIDIT

Us cavaliers si jazia

A knight once lay beside and with
    the one he most desired,
and in between their kisses said,
    what shall I do, my sweet?
Day comes and the knight goes
        Ai!
And I hear the watcher cry :
    'Up! On your way!
    I see day
coming on, sprouting behind the dawn!'

    Sweetheart, if it could be,
and would be never dawn nor day,
what a deliverance it would be
    to happy lovers anywhere
in bed and doing what they please
        Ai!
And I hear the watcher cry :
    'Up! On your way!
    I see day
coming on, sprouting behind the dawn!'

    My beauty, never believe it's so
if it's said there is a dolor
    like the parting of a lover
from his love. Well I know
    night fell a moment ago
        Ai!
And now I hear the watcher cry :
    'Up! On your way!
    I see day
coming on, sprouting behind the dawn!'

    Soft one, I take my way
but yours, no matter where I be.

195

Please God, do not forget me.
This heart is wracked from my body
and forever, will not part from yours
    Ai!
Now I hear the watcher cry :
   'Up! On your way!
   I see day
coming on, sprouting behind the dawn!'

   Dear one, it'd be my death
were I far from where you breathe.
Desire would strike me in the path
   for I've no life without you.
I'll be back, I'll be back soon . . .
    Ai!
   hear it! hear the watcher cry :
   'Up! On your way!
   I see day
coming on, sprouting behind the dawn!'

Partimen

Savaric de Mauleon:

Gaucelm, three plays of love
I'll divide with you and Hugo.
Each of you take whatever pleases
And leave me whichever one you care to.
A lady has three gallant lovers
And with their loves they press her hard:
And when all three are there before her
To each she makes love's semblance.
At one she casts an amorous glance,
Squeezes the second's hand, the third,
She presses his foot and smiles. Now,
Since one is so, tell me in which
Move she shows the greatest love.

Gaucelm Faidit:

Savaric, you know too well, which
Friend received the kindest gift.
No lies, frankly it was the one
Who from her eyes took loving glance.
It's from the heart such softness moves,
Her love's a hundred times better shown.
For, as far as holding hands goes,
I say she meant neither good nor harm
From a mutual pleasure that's so common.
Why, a lady would do as much in greeting.
As for the foot, don't think it's proof
That the lady was making love to him.
If you took it for love you'd be mistaken.

Uc de la Bacalaria:

Say what you will, Gaucelm, you're
Crazy man, you're so far off,
For a glance I know no gain
To a lover—as you claim,
And if he thinks so, he's mad.
The eye regards others—and him,
It has no other power than this.
How much more when, ungloved, the white
Hand squeezed her lover's softly!   Then
Love moved both from the heart and sense.
Since I'm maintaining the noblest part
En Savaric, the polite pressure
Of a foot I can scarcely credit.

Savaric de Mauleon:

Uc, you've left the best to me, so
I'll uphold it and not say no.
I say the gentle pressure given
By her foot was the surest proof:
She hid her fine love from gossiping.
And best, while she gave such heaven
To her lover, she smiled, rejoicing.
Now *that* is love, and undisguised!
Whoever thinks the hand's caress
Shows greater love just makes no sense.
Gaucelm, it doesn't seem to me that .
You can equate a glance with it if
You know love as well as you claim.

Gaucelm Faidit:

Whoever demeans the glances of eye
And the pleasure that may be made thereby,
Doesn't recognize the messengers of the heart

That sends them. They are, assuredly,
For the eyes discover to the lover
What timid hearts keep under cover;
Thus they show *all* of love's pleasure.
But in jest and laughing, a lady often
Will nudge the feet of many men
Without any other understanding.
Uc maintains a fallacy when
He claims the hand is such a treasure.
I say it is not worth a glove.
I bet he's never been moved by love.

Uc de la Bacalaria:

Gaucelm, against Love you've been
Outspoken, the lord of Mauleon too,
And does it ever show in the argument!
For, the eyes, which you have chosen,
Have fooled many a faithful lover.
As for a lady with faithless heart
If she stepped on my foot for a year
My heart would have no rejoicing. But
The hand is beyond contention, for that
Moment of tension is better than either.
If it had not been Love that moved her
Heart, she'd not have put her hand there.

Savaric de Mauleon:

Gaucelm, you've lost the argument,
You and Uc both, indisputably.
And I would have make judgment
Mos-Garda-Cors who's conquered me,
And lady Marie where price frequents.

Gaucelm Faidit:

Vanquished? I sir? By no means,
And the judge shall make it all too plain.
And I wish might be that same
The lady Guillema de Benauges
With her courteous, loving words.

Uc de la Bacalaria:

Gaucelm, I've argued in such degree
That both of you are outside, and I
Sustained. I know a heart so good
In which the judgment may be put,
I've more gain there than any three.

AIMERIC DE PEGUILHAN

(c. 1195—1230)

VIDA

Aimeric de Peguilhan was from Toulouse, the son of a merchant who sold fabrics. He learned cansos and sirventes, but sang very badly. Then he fell in love with a lady of the town, a neighbor of his. It was this love that taught him to sing and compose, and he made many good cansos for her. But he got into difficulties with the lady's husband who humiliated him. En Aimeric avenged himself and hit him in the head with a sword. For which reason it seemed suitable that he leave Toulouse.

He went down to Catalunya and was made welcome by Guillem de Berguedan. In the first canso he made for Guillem his trobar improved. Guillem made him a joglar, gave him clothing and a horse, and presented him to King Alfons of Castile, who enriched Aimeric in equipment and in honor.

He stayed in those parts for a long time, then he came up to Lombardy, where all the catharists paid him great honor. And in Lombardy ended his life.

RAZO

As luck would have it, the lady's husband's wound healed, and he went down to St. James de Compostella. When Aimeric heard the news, he wanted to get back to Toulouse. He went to the king and said that, if it were agreeable to him, he would like to visit the marquis of Montferrat. The king granted his request wholeheartedly and set him well in equipment and all. Then Aimeric told the king that he'd like to pass through Toulouse, but in fact he was apprehensive, for he was aware that the king knew the whole situation, and would see that it was love for his lady that was dragging at him. But the king said nothing and provided him with company as far as Montpellier. Once on the road, he told his companions the whole story so that they would help him, for he wanted to see the lady under the guise of an invalid. And they replied that they would do everything that he asked.

When they got to Toulouse, his companions asked for the inn that the burgher owned and were given directions. When they found the lady, they told her that a cousin of the king of Castile had been taken ill on pilgrimage and would like to take lodgings there. She answered that at the inn he would be served and honored.

Aimeric came that night, and his companions carried him up and put him in a handsome bed. The next day Aimeric sent for the lady. She came into the room, recognized him, and was greatly shocked. She asked him how he could have gotten into Toulouse. And he said through love. Then Aimeric recounted the whole story to her. The lady prepared a screen and hung drapes over it, and kissed him.

Beyond this point, I don't know what happened. But en Aimeric stayed for a full 10 days in that house under the pretext of illness. When he left, he went from here to the marquis where he was well-received. And here you will find some of his work.

Mantas vetz sui enqueritz

At court I'm asked so much I'm sick
how come it is I make no vers, or
how I want to call a piece.
I leave to every man his choice
if this song be canson or vers.
And, to answer the question,
man knows no way, nor has devised a stick
except the name, to tell a vers from canson.

I've heard words with masculine rhymes
in cansonetas a lot of times:
and plenty of feminine endings put
to vers that are pleasant and well-made.
And with many vers I've listened
to tortuous notes, terse and short.
And I've heard cansons with long, even tunes, and
both with hard words where the song's a single note.

If they call me a liar, well?
what I've said may not be true:
I'll curse out no man whatsoever
if, in the right, he contradict me.
Rather, his reputation would swell
and mine be lessened in the court,
if, with sound reason, he can beat me at it,
for I hardly have all of Solomon's wit.

Courtship, which used to be so highly
prized, is gone from its proper place;
myself, I've turned away from Love
some little, so painful is his face
to look at—what's between loved and lover
these days is manifest deceit,
for one and the other thinks that by deceit he'll profit,
and doesn't care when, where, how, or with whom he does it.

For I saw, before Love's rough
dismissal, if a cordon were given
for love's sake, it was enough—
close conversation was not finished
and only the rich invited in.
Having made it on both sides of the wash,
it seems to me a year's not equal
to a month when Love reigned without business deals.
Hard to see how it stands nowadays, and know how it was.

Although I'm not in love presently,
I've not abandoned him totally,
but I would not fall in love even with
someone the top and root of price, if
it were not to my good. When
true valor and the semblance
of it are assembled in
such one fine fashioning a man can say that
he cannot think of a better, then okay.

Gently nursed and precious one,
straight, well-fashioned, you may guess
what I want to say to you. I'm
hardly that bold I could ask you
that you love me just like that,
before begging mercy and thankful for it.
Permit me to love you—I ask no other gift, and
sure you must understand and honor that petition.

To the Malaspina, go, my song
& see the valiant, worthy William
so that he learns from you the words and tune,
whether he wants to call you vers or cansoun.

Beatrice Este, you've pleased me now
for a good long time—that's no small thing.
Since all good men are busy with your praise
I shall take you to gild my canso-vers.

Can que·m fezes vers ni canso

As much as I've made vers and canso,
now I want just words, no tune,
for a lady's found fault with me;
that gets me upset and confused.
She spoke rebukingly and begged me
to quit both song and courting, said
I was too tired for lover's work!
But had she thoroughly perused

my qualities, don't think she'd've dared
say that, the heart—at least—is there.
I can tell evil from goodness, and
native-wit from foolishness;
I know how to be thankful for, of course,
whoever gives me comfort and honor,
and to pay back good for good and
evil for evil, if I'm forced.

I'm skillful in still other ways:
know how to hold goodness in esteem
and to fear and doubt the wicked, I'm
that subtle quick adroit and sharp.
I can go or I can come,
take dalliance or suffer pain,
am sensitive to heat or cold
being closer-shaved than anyone.
Among sophisticates I've learned
to entertain with graceful words
but not to pleasure all equally.
Discretion's the word in company.

And with the good ladies I know well
what it's fitting to say or tell,
and when I answer, guard my tongue
from a word that could be taken wrong.
When wars break out and battles rise

I get into my armor by myself
alone—I don't shorten the straps.
Then I'm horsed and armored to the eyes.

And when I'm mounted up and ready
I make him feel the spur and whip
until it makes him swift and lively.
And when my destrier's well-mastered,
and I'm up and armored and set,
only Hector and Tydeus compare
with me. No one makes two passes
as quick as I do in emergency.

I've pierced many a shield and escutcheon,
split it down the middle with my lance,
& have struck down & 've been struck down,
and've fallen and got to my feet again.
And don't imagine I stay down long,
I'm back in the saddle right away.
And I joust better the second day
than I did the first, by heaven.

And in combat I use the maces
equally mightily, such strokes
the noise they make alone spreads terror
when they crack down on shield and buckler.
I fight like a lion, am that bold
I come out fine from the stiffest stour,
return with cheer and joust some more,
so I think she's wrong to call me old.

But if on foot or horseback either
the lady will do combat with me,
do battle with me as a test
I wouldn't hold I'd been ill-judged.

Messenger, carry my flabel
there to la Marca to en Sordel,
who will make the new decision
with his usual justice and precision
if here I've acquitted myself, and well.

GAVAUDAN

(c. 1195—1230)

No existing vida.

Lo vers dech far

This vers I make
or should
on such rhymes,
masculine
& feminine,
that it rhyme well.
Grain,
I screen it
from the straw
in such a way
that no one could mix them again. Hell,
I can set in the balance as well this
empty frivolous crowd who turn
what's soft to bitter by their thin
bitter love.
Watch an ember
grow to a bonfire when
already dead in appearance, it
takes fire again.

When it's a good vine
that produces, then
one loves the grape.
That much one
who's well-aligned
should love his lady, provided
she keeps to the rules and doesn't go sleeping around.
If she tells
you she's never
loved another,
be a fool, believe it.
And when your joy abandons you
be twice as glad of the treason.
And you lovers,
you idiots,

you gulls!
are you so stupid as to believe you can
tame these women of their petulant wills?

Understand,
she who plays hide-the-salami
with two men
will find it hard
to refuse the game to a third: you see
now why Joy is in trouble?
Indeed,
no one troubles himself. So .
Some goat puts the husband in a sack that
smells like stale water from a camel's back;
and she'll stand and watch him fill it up
from a full bladder.
But, she *will* make a nasty face,
for she offers no one the chance
of having mastery over her.

False Love knows scrimmaging so well that
he who scrimmages
not against him
is as sure of a greater
clap of battle's thunder later
as a bell is sure of its clapper striking sometime.
"Fool,"
she'll say, "leave off your preaching,
you've taken me for an owl too long.
Be cheap and niggardly toward me, toward
you my avarice'll be unparalleled!"
And sure, then nothing good will be
lacking to him, until
she sets him in a fever again . . .

I am so delicate
and prim

with lady Grim
that never would I wish to make her
grim toward me.
O,
she complains
(her pains)
she groans and
moans, she even
yawns,
and even yawning is one of her tricks,
for she makes
a sodden fool
of the wisest man with a roll.
And when she has his wallet and wealth, she
"no longer deigns to admit him"
and looks around for another gull to admit who has
a wallet and name
whom she can make equally sick.

What is so soft to begin with
can, by pointed and subtle engineering
pierce a good hauberk of stout mail,
leg-guard, gloves of steel, helm
as well.
She knows her latin
and greek so nice
she could sell
herself as a greek abbess.
And there is no defense against her, she
betrays all who protect her.
She turns one eye and winks the other,
the reliability of a sieve.
And the engine steamrolls over the naive.

Integrity demands one have a file
to make the prison-break in style.
Me,

where's trouble? I clear out of the way.
Her devotees are always in trouble, be they
old or young.
Nero who murdered Seneca
had a heart like hers,
sincere,
near the lung.
False Love never opens her heart
or reveals to those who
to her reveal their own,
though it be sung out,
though she swear and promise to do it.

More than a bullock labors,
I cudgel my head to labor and break
this crime open.
Those she cannot chew or sell,
she'll see they're broken.

But the vers is good
if it's written well.

I'll launch it like a ship on the wave.
May there be wind and the signs favorable.
I hope King Anfos will act as helm
winter and summer
breeze and gale .

PONS DE CAPDUEILL

(c. 1196 : d. before 1236)

VIDA

Pons de Capdueill was from the same bishopric as Guillem de St. Leider. He was a rich man, a very noble baron, expert at composing and playing the viol, and sang well. He was skilled at arms and a good conversationalist, pleasing when he courted the ladies, big, handsome, and well-educated, and very short on cash; but he made up for this by a warm welcome and giving freely the honor of his presence.

He loved dearly ma domna Azalais de Mercuor, wife of en Oisil de Mercuor and daughter of Bernart d'Andusa, an honored baron from the March of Proensa. He loved her well and praised her, and made many good cansos for her. He loved no other as long as she lived, and when she died, he took the cross and went to fight overseas, where he died. And here is written down one of his cansos.

RAZO

As you heard before, Pons de Capdueill loved ma dona Azalais de Mercuor, wife of an important Auvergnat count and daughter of en Bernart d'Andusa. She loved him very much, and their love was esteemed by all good people. Many fair courts and fine jousts were held, many good times were had because of it, and many fine cansos made on that account.

Being in that esteem with her, having this happiness and desiring it so, like a maddened lover who has not known and cannot stand sudden success, he asked her if she loved him, for he did not believe his eyes, nor could he trust the charming kindnesses and the overwhelming honor she paid him by her acts and her speech. He decided in his crazy heart that he would pretend to court another lady, N'Audiart, who was wife of the lord of Marseille. So he did, thinking that, if his lady were grieved at his absenting himself from her, he would know that she truly was in love with him; and should it please her, it would be a good proof that she did not love him. So, like the fool who would not yield until the wound was in him, he started to stay away from ma dona Azalais and come on to ma dona Audiart and to speak well of her, for he says:

> I wouldn't want to be
> emperor of Germany
> if my eyes could not see
> Audiart.
> Too much, but if she saw me gay and asked me to undress,
> I'd ask nothing but that my company please her.

Ma dona Azalais, when she saw that Pons de Capdueill, whom she had loved and honored so, had left her and gone to ma dona Audiart, she had only great contempt, and she never asked for him or spoke to anyone about him; nor did she answer anyone who spoke of it to her. She lived on with a splendid court and continued to receive admirers.

So Pons de Capdueill went courting over in Provence for a long while, fleeing the honors ma dona Azalais had given him. And when he realized that she had not shown any anger nor sent letters or messengers after him, he finally saw that he'd done the wrong thing. Slowly he made his way back to her lands, and disengaged himself from the foolish proof he had made. He sent messengers and letters to her, but she would neither accept them or listen to them. He grew sad and was in great pain. He sent letters and humble coblas to her, begging desperately that she allow him to come before her to reason his reasons, and to beg and cry mercy, saying that she should have her vengeance on him if he had offended her. But she would not listen to them, mercy or reason. Then he made the canso which goes:

> If like someone who has a sufficiency
> of helpful friends.

And this canso got him nowhere with the lady, and he made another which starts:

> Anyone who swallows foolishly
> everything she hears
> is making a big mistake,
> it has to turn out to hurt.

And this one was equally valueless, for though ma dona Azalais wanted to return him to favour, she did not want to believe that he had left her and stayed away just to prove her, to see if she would be happy or not if he left her. At this juncture, he went to Maria de Ventadorn, the countess of Montferrat, and the viscountess of Albuisson, and he brought them to Mercuor to Azalais, to cry mercy that she would grant him grace. And she did it out of affection for the ladies. Then Pons de Capdueill was the happiest man in the world, and swore that he would never again do anything to have proof of his lady.

And here is written one of his cansos having to do with this razo, as you shall hear.

Qui per nesci cuidar

Anyone who swallows foolishly
everything she hears
is making a big mistake,
it has to turn out to hurt.
And if, mistaking me,
even my lady puts me down,
it's well deserved,
for such craziness as I have shown,
the depression and fury alone
are enough to kill me.

And if I have been over-bitter and acted a damn fool
shall I now verify with my lady that I am sacked?
and that she'd rejoice in her heart
if that firm will which I have to serve her
were to depart?
No matter that now I'm cool I
know what would please her,
I might as well cut out my tongue,
it would not appease her.
I have played the ass too long.

I know it's not right
still I can't keep my head
. . . if she wants to pardon me
with both hands.
I render her thanks forever.
Anything else, she kills me
now my heart is sure and won't leave
the rich place where he immovably
stands.

It's not even important
if that rich, handsome body of hers
deceive me,

but she doesn't have to turn from me
because everyone's making so much noise.
For I'm a man, thank God, and know
there's not a better one to have
for gallantry
or solace.

Yet I stand singing for myself alone,
a damn fool in heart and sense.
I think I'm going to stand on pride
and she flattens me.
My body humbles itself towards her
she won't give me the time of day;
neither Love nor his rules pay nor
get me joy of her.

Lady, loveliest I know—
no conceit or falsity—
I love you better than
Tristan his Iseult and
I've nothing for it.

JAUSBERT DE PUYCIBOT

(c. 1210—1230)

VIDA

The monk Jausbert de Puycibot was a wellborn man from the bishopric of Limoges, son of a castellan of Puycibot. When he was still a child he was made a monk and entered in a monastery called Saint Leonart. He was well-versed in letters and knew how to sing and compose.

And out of desire for women he left the monastery and went where anyone went who wished for honor and bounty through *cortesia*, to en Savaric de Malleon, who gave him a joglar's harness, clothing and horses. Then he went through all the courts and composed and made good cansos.

He fell in love with a lovely and noble young lady (*donzella*) and made his cansos to her. But she did not wish to love him unless he became a knight and took her to wife. He told en Savaric how the young lady had refused him; then en Savaric knighted him and gave him land and rents. So he married the girl and held her in great honor.

And it happened he went down to Spain and the young lady stayed behind. An English knight fell in love with her, and did and talked so much that he ended by taking her with him on the road and kept her for a long time as his mistress. Finally he maltreated her and left her to go her own way.

When Jausbert was returning from Spain, he put up one night in the city where she was. And when evening came he went out looking for a woman and entered the inn of a poor woman who told him she had a beautiful young girl inside. He found his wife. When they saw each other it was very painful for both of them, and great shame. He spent the night with her, and the next morning he took her to a convent and entered her in it. And for this grief he ceased to sing and compose.

And here is written one of his cansos.

Be·s cujet venjar amors

BECAUSE I HAD REPROACHED HIM where he failed,
Love intended to take his vengeance on me by
     leaving me suddenly.
     But if he wanted to,
he couldn't have done me more honor.
Now I feel neither dolor nor pain,
I don't even complain,
and I was getting used to complaining.
But now take more enjoyment, having
gathered back at Love's parting, the
     loose ends of my wit,
the spirit he'd taken from me at his coming,
     I'd
     recovered my pride.

     I was filled with such insanity,
     Love so compelled my wit
     I was thoroughly taken in by and loved fully
     a cold, ungrateful bitch whom I believed
          was the flower of beauty
     and had dominion, was the top of valor.
     Well, I've had enough of her nonsense.
     A man should choose a woman who
     makes herself worthy of praise.
     Luckily I have no booking-agent.
     The road's straight
          and I know how to put
     one foot in front of the other.

But a true lover *has to* believe his lady can do no wrong,
and if she does the wrong, it makes no matter.
Better he take the shame to have been an honor,
and any light-blown whim as ultimate sense.
So long as I loved her wholly
I praised her with words of which she was not worthy.

If I was guilty
of mendacity
now I speak the truth, make no mistake,
to pay the lie I told myself as well.

No other way to scrub the stain of a lie
but by the sound of truth.
Well, let's hear it!
I was a true lover and praised her,
she was not worth it.
I know that will cut somewhat,
but I want to come at a verity
to temper the fault.

My body did not turn elsewhere, I
loved so well.
My praise told
everyone her worth in my eyes.
I refused to believe the stories
the whole world else knew were true,
and went on praising a valor and price
she did not possess.
As far as that goes, I've nothing to deny
of the fine things I said I witnessed there.
I thought I spoke the truth. It's only fair
to point out the not-so-fine discrepancy between hallucination and verity.

Lady,
if I continue discussing this nonsense in my songs,
and you continue to act it out
before long
you'll be undone completely.
I can see both of us working at the destruction,
I by my words and you with action.

CADENET

(first half of 13th C.)

VIDA

Cadenet was from Provence, from a castle called Cadenet on the banks of the Durance in the county of Forcalquier, and was the son of a poor knight. When he was still a child, the castle of Cadenet was sacked and destroyed by the people of the count of Toulouse, killing the men of the land or taking them prisoner. He himself was led into the Toulousain by a knight named Guillem de Lantar who brought him up and kept him in his house. He grew to be fine, handsome and courteous, knew how to compose and sing, was good at conversation, and learned to compose coblas and sirventes.

When he left the lord who had brought him up, he became a joglar and went through all the courts; and he had himself called Baguas. For a long time he went under an evil star on foot about the world. And he came back to Provence and no man knew him. Then he changed his name to Cadenet and began to make good and beautiful cansos. En Raimon Leugier of the Two Brothers castle in the

222

bishopric of Nice gave him fine raiment and great honor. En Blancatz honored him and showed him much favor.

For a very long time he had great possessions and great honor. Then he entered the Hospitallers, and there died. All these facts about him I knew by hearsay and by seeing myself.

S'anc fui belha ni prezada

Once I was lovely, had renown,
now certainly, I've been brought down.
I was given to a clod because
he had more money than God.
        I'd have died
had I not had a lover beside
where I could pour out my chagrin.
        The guard served well
who called out it was dawn.

Now, I'm the gentle guardian.
I don't want loyal love undone
        that's only taken
what is its right alone.
So I guard against the dawn
        lest it come.
She who lies with lover, how
openly she takes their parting,
        kissing close
when I cry out, seeing dawn.

To please me give me a long dark night
the coldest winter you can imagine,
let the Garonne freeze, I'll be here.
A faithful guard's in trust forever
        so they may rest secure.
A good lover taking his joy and pleasure
        of a lady of valor
        wants to be at it
        night till dawn.

If I stood sentry-go in fortress where
only lustful, only false love thrived,
I'd be false if I didn't hide the dawn
        as often as I could.

For I'd want
to put an end
to base love-making
in that court
but here serve loyally, cry
out when I see dawn.

Not for mockery or the threats
that my evil husband makes me
would I change my way : I lie
with my lover until day.
For it'd be
a most arrogant villeiny
to part from one's lover
roughly
before dawn.

I've never seen any
horizontal lover
who liked dawn.

Likewise it seems abrupt to me.
I also,
I hate to see
dawn come up.

SORDELLO

(c. 1225—1270)

VIDA

I.

Sordello was from Cereda near Mantua, son of a poor knight named Curtus. And it gave him great pleasure to learn cansos and to compose them. And he rubbed elbows with the Cathars in the court, learning everything he could, and he made coblas and sirventes.

He came to the court of the count of St. Bonifaci and the count honored him greatly. He became enamoured of the count's wife, as a form of diversion, and she with him. And it happened that the count was on bad terms with her brothers and grew very cool with her. Her brothers, Sir Aicelin and Sir Albric, had Sordello steal her from the count, and he went to stay with them. He stayed with them for a long time and in great happiness.

And then he went over into Provence where he received great

226

honor from all the Cathars and from the count and the countess, who gave him a good castle and a noble wife.

II.

Sordello was from Mantua, from a castle called Goito. A noble castellan by birth, he was a handsome man in his person, a good singer, a good troubadour, and a great lover. But he was very faithless toward the ladies, and false to those barons with whom he lived.

He fell in love with Cunizza da Romano, sister of Aicelin and Albric da Romano, who was married to the count of St. Bonifaci with whom Sordello was staying. And because Sir Aicelin wanted it so, he stole Cunizza and ran off with her.

A little afterwards he went into the Cenedese to a castle of the Estras, Enric, Guillem, and Valpertin, who were good friends of his, and he married a sister of theirs, Otha, secretly. Later he left for Treviso alone. When the Estras found out they wanted to do him personal violence, and the friends of the count of St. Bonifaci likewise. For which reason Sordello stayed in the house of Sir Aicelin and kept arms by him. When he went through the countryside, he rode good horses and with a large company of knights.

For Fear of those who wanted to get him, he left and went into Provence and stayed with the count of Provence. He loved a beautiful lady of that country, and in the cansos which he made for her he called her "Doussa-Enemia" (The Gentle Enemy); for which lady he made many good cansos.

Planher vuelh en Blacatz en aquest leugier so

SIMPLY, IT IS A MAN who has died:
this light song must bear the weight
of that death
and my grief:
a bitter song, for I have lost
master and friend,
and all worth has gone down with him to death.
Here, only my mortal pain, and in this world
no hope that worth be restored, except
          his heart be drawn
and that these princely pigeons eat of it.

Since he has the greatest need of it,
the Roman Emperor should be the first
          to eat of it
if he wants to conquer the Milanese by force.
          They're sure he's beaten, have already
run him off his claim and licked his Germans.

                    The King of Castile—
                    better he eat for two.
                    He holds two kingdoms
                    and has not valor for one.
                    If he wants a taste, he'll
                    have to chew it in private.
                    If his mother finds out
                    she'll beat him with a club.

The King of England pleases me
for he is a little courageous.
If he ate enough of the heart he might
          have valor enough to recover
the territory France stole, wherein
he is stripped of honor.

I wish the King of Aragon to grace the table,
for only so can he free himself from the shame
in which he is held this side of Marseille and Aveyron:
as it stands, no man can honor his words or deeds.

And now a man called king and worth as little
as when he was called count,
the King of Navarre.
I wouldn't know what to call him.
God raised him to great power—behold,
the non-descript.

The Count of Toulouse might recall
with a reasonable portion,
that he used to be the ruler, not the ruled.
If another's heart will not retrieve his loss
the one in his chest will avail his people nothing.

The Count of Provence, having tasted the heart of Blancatz,
might remember a man is not worth a glove
robbed of his birthright.
He bears a great burden,
has need of a brave man's heart,
until he holds his ground
and defends himself.

The barons will wish me ill-fortune, for I speak straight:
but they know I prize them as little as they do me.

Fair Healer, with whom alone
I may find mercy,
scorn each one
who holds me not a friend.

AIMERIC DE BELENOI

(c. 1217—1242)

VIDA

Aimeric de Belenoi was from the Bordelais, from a castle called Lesparra, and was the nephew of maistre Peire de Corbiac. He was a clerk turned joglar, and made good cansos, beautiful ones, graceful ones, for a lady from Gascoigne named Gentils de Rius. For her sake he stayed for a long time in that country. Then he went into Catalunya and remained there until he died. And here is written down one of his cansos.

Nulhs hom no pot cumplir addreichamen

No man can utterly fulfill what he has in his heart
but when he does it, it
seems but a little thing.
When he is satisfied his love is perfect
his heart proves the defect.
Thought of perfection can only bring him down
                    in the performance.
No so for me, I swear
to her I hold most
close, most dear,
it must be someone loves her better than I
who think myself able to love her but little.

Set against my comprehension of it,
my thought,
my love makes a poor showing.
Honors, goods,
more than I have love for her, I have not, knowing
if I could love her as she merits it
                    I would be King of Love!
of Youth, of all fine fact and rich!
Yet no one can have honor equal
to true merit and its worth.
                    The full rich fact remains
that my heart in its clumsiness cannot fulfill.
So I suffer
a pain so great
it should be credited me as feat
having borne, having overborne it.

He who wants to, and cannot, act
has agony
a hundred times worse than his
who can and does.
The fact. For power

puts fear down, wins from
the man whose power it is, all grief,
all soreness of love.
        Such fences.
But she where hope is has such excellences
that she knows how by
a delicacy
to draw all merit to her.
Thus she guards herself in loving. Nor
has she ever made an issue of the edge,
        the having,
        the not-having.

When I set her graceful body within my heart
the soft thought there is so agreeable, I
sicken, I burn for joy,
and loving her more passionately than ever, I
die of desire,
wanting to love her more, wanting
my love to grow so great
that I can die of it
        or she take pity.
    For joy of love, even when the lady grants it,
can only mount so much as one desires her.

A gift is worth, not more, than the receiver of it.
Its limits are the pleasure that he proves.
Thus my hope in part:
for if my lady thinks of the joy I'll take
of her precious gifts, if
mercy gains her heart
        (otherwise nothing stands)
mercy and she
will come to firm agreement. For it's mercy
makes a hard rich heart draw near
a loyal heart put down from over-love.

Go song, toward the lovely Eleanor.
Near her even perfection betters itself.
And I send you there to improve yourself, hear?
And if she makes you a fine welcome
walk full of confidence and cheer.

But if she does not give the script a passing glance,
go burn yourself,
                    and do not fear the heat.

BERNART ARNAUT DE MONCUC

(first quarter of the 13th C.)

No existing vida.

Er quan li rozier

Now, when the rozier blows
without seed or blossom,
and the rich miser hunting, goes
in the quaggy meadows,
I am sunk in thought.
It pleases me to quarrel
and to make sirventes:
for all good values are
held in contempt & scorn.
 And because I
 am kept more gay
by Love than I was ever
by the fine May weather,
today I'm gay, whomever it depress,
such joy can be given by a promise.

Many a fast horse we
see heading up Tarzana
and toward Balaguier.
The valorous king who goes there
whose mark is greater than any,
 'll come without failing
up to Carcassonne: no,
hardly greater trembling
not even the French have.
 More of you
 I've not, I know
Lady. It makes me groan
the full desire I have
for your graceful, handsome body, clad
and surfilled with all good.

The armored destrier and
the hauberk, the smooth lance,
plus a good steel sword

and approaching war,
is better by far than training
    greyhounds how to dance,
    or living like a heifer
    in a peace in which a man
    is diminished of his land,
    brought down, humiliated.
        And I know
        values true
    in you whom I shall have
    or else dig my grave,
who, forbid, are more to me forever
    than if I had another.

The archer has a cheerful manner
    standing next the loop-hole
when he draws on the stone-gunner
    & loses the parapet wall.
    While past many orchards
    the army grows & shines:
    such maintenance I'd like
    right well to undertake
    there to the English king.
        So I am blunt
        when I recount
    how you give me joy
    young lady, here & now.
Beauty aside, your valor's overwhelming
    since you lack in nothing.

And I'd have that integrity entire
    that everyone despises,
    with such git & fire
    as you cry there, "GUIANA!"
And I shall be the first the count
    decorates for valor.
    His sealed communiqués

take so little time to read,
them I'll scarcely mention.
　　Yet I'll say
　　but with fear
　　I'm in love.
　　Lady, what to do?
if mercy for me won't obtain with you
　　or my good faith?
　　Who, senher,
　　who in truth
knows how to honor each
disputant? I say I know the catch,
　　Toulousain or Agenes,
　　despite the French.

MONTANHAGOL

(c. 1233—1270)

VIDA

Guillem de Montanhagol was a knight from Provence, and he was a good troubadour and a great lover. He fell in love with ma domna Jauseranda from the castle of Lunel, and made many good cansos for her.

Del tot vey remaner valor

On all sides I see valor pull up short,
for no one anywhere these days
takes the trouble. I
don't overhear one fine thought a month. All
their hearts are most concerned with is
        profit.
When clerks and frères prêcheurs legislate
against what doesn't suit them, that
        proves their merit?
    For an instance:

    PROHIBITED
Any man (caring for honor) to give gifts
    or be otherwise liberal.

I'd question the basis of anyone's motives who
blackens generosity and misprizes honor.

God intended man to have his praise and price.
He made man noble and powerful,
shaped him closer to Himself than
to any other thing living. So,
how can anyone counter His design?
A man is mad not to respect himself. Let him
act in this world so that he have
some gratification in this world
        and that other world,
wherever there be some to have.

As it stands, the clerks
set themselves up as inquisitors
and judge according to their caprice.
It isn't that the
        INQUISITION
            displeases me,

on the contrary,
I really enjoy watching them hunt down error,
                especially
the dispassionate and a-, persuasive discourse
with which they lead strayed heretics back to the faith.
I would also approve if, when one repented,
one also found pardon;
                and if the inquisitors worked
                in such a way as to respect
                the RIGHTS
(especially the property rights) of
the just as well as the unjust.

And they're talking complete idiocy when they pretend
gold stuffs do not suit the ladies.
Say that a lady does not sin,
has no conceit of herself
and is not proud,
she'll go to hell
and lose God's love—
what? by dressing well?
Everything else being equal,
God's not offended by their dressing up a bit.
Do you think it's because of black vestments and white surplices
                the priests'll conquer heaven, having
                done nothing else to merit it?

                For God's love our clerks renounce this perverse time,
                and all their thought is on the life to come. Fine.
                God keep them from dishonor as long as
                they're without pride or riches,
                so long as they don't stray and covet all
                the beautiful things they see around.
                You know, they desire nothing, but isn't it curious,
                they always cart everything off?
                And they don't give a tinker's damn
                if anyone's hurt by it.

Go, sirventes, to Toulouse, let
the valiant count remember what
the clerks have done against him.
From now on, may he not be loose
but keep his eye peeled for them.

PEIRE CARDENAL

(c. 1225—1272?)

VIDA

Peire Cardenal was from Veillac, the city of Puy. The son of a knight and a lady, he was of good parentage, and when he was small, his parents entered him as a canon in the largest canonry in Puy. He learned letters and became accomplished at reading and singing.

When he had come to the state of manhood, he took pleasure in the vanity of this world, for he felt himself gay and handsome and young. He made many handsome arguments and handsome songs, and he made cansos but not many. He made a lot of sirventes, very fine ones, in which he set forth many good arguments and fine examples which I well understand; for he scourged mightily the follies of this world, often reproaching the false clerks, as accordingly his sirventes show.

And he went through the courts of kings and noble barons, bringing a joglar with him who sang his sirventes. He was highly esteemed and honored by the good King Jacme of Aragon and by many famous barons.

And I, maistre Miquel de la Tor, here writing, do testify that en Peire Cardenal when he passed from this life was nearly a hundred years old. And I, the above-said Miquel, have written down these sirventes in the city of Nîmes.

And here are written some of his sirventes.

Tan son valen nostre vezi

Our neighbors are so courteous, worthy and human!
    If stones were bread
    and water were wine
and mountains were salt pork and chicken meat
    they still wouldn't be generous.
    There *are* people like that.

And there are those, but I name them not, who'd be
        pigs in Gavaudan,
        borzois in the Viennois
        and, at Velay, would
        sings at matins:
in short, perfect dogs—only the tail lacking.

In the oaths of women, no, I have no faith,
nor would I ask them to swear anything to me,
        for put
a marabotin in one hand to tell the truth
and a garlic in the other to pay a lie and
        you know already,
        zut! the garlic wins.

Then there are those who pretend to be infants, but
    are as smart as the lawyer Trebellius,
who've the verbal talents of logicians combined
    with all the goodwill of a wolf,
those who under a handsome body, blessed with
fine blond hair, hide humbug, lying hearts.

    I should have to speak like a Saracen,
        gilded and fired,
have all the power of Christian faith and law,
        pagan subtility,
    and the courage of a Tartar to be

well-outfitted enough to be
  a castilian liar.

But go ahead, do wickedness, tell lies!
Just as if there weren't enough already.

Li clerc si fan pastor

The clerks pretend to be shepherds, and under
    a show of sanctity are
    ravening cut-throats.
When I see one shimmy into a cassock, I
think of Alengri the wolf,
who thought to break into
                the sheep-cote but
        was afraid on account of the mastiffs . . .
    but then he had an idea.
He pulled a sheepskin over his head
and ate as much as he liked.

Kings
emperors
dukes
counts
& knights
used to rule the world.
Now priests have the power, got
by robbery, treachery, sermons, force and hypocrisy.
And they're quite annoyed when all
the land's not left them.
    No matter what the terms are, they'll
    get it, by taking—or giving.
        (Thy Will Be Done. Sure.)

    The higher in rank they are
    the less they are in valor.
    The more ecstatic they seem
    the more they lie
and less frequent is the sound of solid truth.
The less they monk the more they sin
and the less they like each other for it—Christ!
    these false clerks!

Such efficient enemies God's never had
    this side of antiquity.

When they sit together in refectory,
    I don't see it
    as simple honor
    that tradesmen
            sit at the highest table
            getting the choice cuts,
            shoulder, haunch—
            hear the baseness!
They've nerve, I'll tell you that, and come and go
where they please
and no man dare
deny them place
    whereat to set their paunches.
But one thing I've never seen, and that's
    a poor mendicant cuss sitting
            on a bench
            next the rich
            taking lunch.
    That you must excuse them.

The Alcays and Almassors
and other Moslems need not fear
they'll be attacked by abbot or prior
and their land seized.
    That's too much like work.
        But here they study how to best
        subdue the world to their own use
        or put Frederick off his stride.
        But such a one attacked him of late
        as did not get much joy from it.

Clerks, if a man think
to best you at any swindle,

and take you in with
wicked heart and
treacherous mind,
he'll never make the same mistake again.
    I swear I've never seen
such a cut-throat bunch of businessmen!

Tos temps azir falsetat et enjan

Truth and right are my bases.
　　I hate frauds and hypocrites. And
　　　　if I vacillate sufficiently
　　　　　avoiding them,
my rancor sinks, and I find all is well.
　　　　　　Doubtless,
there are those who harm us in honesty,
but there are those too who do it from malice and treachery.
And it happens from time to time
　　a man can climb by falsity
　　　　all the way up the ridge-pole, but
　　　　　it's a long way down.

Rich men, you know, have so
much charity for others,
like Cain had for Abel.
Thievery? They
enjoy it better than any wolf;
as for liars,
you'll find they're more professional than
whores
of the common brothel variety.
Tap them.
You'll not get a drop of truth, though they
run like water from a mountain spring—
mendacity. 90 Proof.

　　　　　I see enough lords in high places
　　　　　like pieces of paste in a ring.
　　　　　　False.
　　　　　And others that claim that these are just
　　　　　are altogether too ready to sell
　　　　　　a wolf for a lamb.
　　　　　　For they cast the denier of Puy
　　　　　　and never strike the legal weight.

You have flowers on it and a cross, but
        melt it down!
You won't find a trace of silver.

I've made a new pact with men
from the east to the setting sun:
every honest man gets a bezant,
and those that are faithless? they get a hobnail each.
If every old hog with his snout in the public trough
        will give me a tornes,
    I offer a gold mark to every man
        with a courtly soul!
I would build a stack of gold for every loyal man
if each scoundrel would give me an egg apiece.

        I could write on a parchment paring
            all of most men's honesty.
        What's there, I could put on my thumb,
            on a *half* of the thumb
                of my glove.
        I could satisfy the hunger of
        all the good men in the world
                with a bun,
            a goddamned cookie would do it.
        Sure it couldn't cost much to feed honest men?
        If you were a man used to feeding thieves, you
        could cry *"Venez!"* at hazard, anywhere,
        "Come on, eat! All of you, you Just of the World!"
        and wait,
            and never see one.

Of those who have worth and virtue in appearance only
I hate hearing it said that they are *worthy*, and *virtuous*.
I hate hearing those men called just
                who laugh at justice.
If they commit evil or outright crimes, they've
            not the right to be welcomed in

with praise and honor.
The saying goes among the people:
"Get burned once. You won't get clipped the second time."

I say to everyone in this text
that if right and truth and mercy
do not govern man in this world,
    I don't see that it helps the values any
        in this world or the next.

Tartarassa ni voutor

Kites and vultures cannot smell out carrion
as readily as clerks and preachers can
a rich man.
They gain his close, & when sickness strikes
he'll make them gifts that his relations
could well use.

Priests and Frenchmen are of ill-repute;
they know too well the game of take-and-run.
Traitors and usurers divide the world among
themselves.
By careful lying, by commercial fraud,
they make the century a turbine funnel
shoveling their gain into the fortress.
        There is no order does not know
        the rate of interest.

Do you know what comes of the riches
of those who have them *malamen*?
A lusty robber will fall on them,
        DEATH, by name,
and with four ells of linen he will pack them off
to a house where they will have their fill of him.

The incredible persistence of
men who are forever flouting
the rule of a reasonable, generous lord
who shaped them out of nothing.
Those who pit themselves against God
get the gull's end of the bargain.
They shall have such guerdon as
Judas had, the felon.

                True God, Lord, full of softness,
                guard, protect from hell's occlusion

all of these unhappy sinners.
Pardon them their cankerous sin,
the condemning chain that binds them,
pardon them with full confession.

PEDRO III OF ARAGON
PEIRE SALVATGE
COUNT OF FOIX
MAESTRE BERNART D'AURIAC

(last half of 13th C.)

P. de ARAGON . P. SALVATGE . C^l de FOIX . BERNART d'AURIAC

Peire Salvatg' en greu pessar

Peire Salvatge, it's the flowers.
Too well I know the heavy smell
of *fleur de lis.*
And what a depressing turn of mind
they give me in this season—
in my own house even,
when I know
these lilies are intent upon invasion. So
I ask the men of Carcassonne,
of Agen and the Gascons also,
that if the flowers spread and hem me in
they give the fact some recognition.
The flowers think to earn a pardon by this invasion,
which pardon they'll find is linked to endless loss
and final perdition.

And now my nephew would like to change
sides,
just to carry some flowers!
I don't think he recognizes me very well
standing under the emblem with the bars,
for we hear tell
he calls himself now king of Aragon.
But no matter who's pleased
or displeased, for that,
with my peasant jacks,
will have to mix it with them when
the onslaughts rise—
please God, may the straightest come for me
for, by the Breton's staff, I'll never
leave the standard where the banner
flies!

Salvatge, if my lady will,
her body full

PEDRO,
king
of
Aragon

255

PEDRO,
king
of
Aragon

of all the noble goods there are and shall
be, may come to credit me,
and may within her body's grace find
some sweet pay,
so long as I gaze upon that lovely face
I'll need no armor against an enemy blade!

*

Riposte
by
PEIRE
SALVATGE

My lord king, an amorous man of decision
shouldn't have a bitter heart against the flowers:
on the contrary,
should envision how he can best, with clarion gusto
pick them,
in this month when summer is
and the flowers spring up luxuriant.
And may the reapers be of such fine pluck, that
picking over plain and mountain, wood and field,
that from here to Monmelian, they'll leave no
flower unplucked.

*

Count
of
Foix

Let no man go to gather flowers
without a stout stick to take.
The French know how to place a swack
and how to aim the pikes they pack.
So don't count on the Carcassonnes
nor the Agenois
nor the Gascons. You know?
since I made my last mistake
they find I can't love anyone?
And soon we'll hear my Burgundians
crying, "Montjoi!"
from *inside* Aragon.

*

Our king, who has no equal for
good fame and nobility,

is going to fly his gonfalon.
Then we'll see by land and sea
the flowers march: and well I know
that, then, some Aragonese will see
what the French are like!
and Catalans bound tight at the knees
by flowers! flowers of honest seed.
and then we'll hear the length of Aragon
"*Oil* and *Nenil*" in place of "*Oc* and *No*"!

Maestre
BERNART   Seems to me that he who swings so hard
D'AURIAC,   and wants to cull the flowers doesn't
clerk   recognize who the gardners are,
of   who just on guard,
Beziers   can line up behind them these so-puissant lords.
             For these gardners make such a threesome
             that each is a king richer than that
             one in Barcelona. And God
             and the Church as well are with them in this fight.
             And let them get down past Canigou
             they'll leave no palace, house nor tower upright.

             Catalans, don't take it hard
             if the French king comes around
             to see you in such handsome harness.
             He only wants to hang you for
             your malversation,
             and absolve you with the lance and pike,
             you've been so long in excommunication.

                                    *

PEDRO   Salvatge, hear them all sing
DE   together, like lovers to the king
ARAGON   of Aragon!
             But tell me, can all that be done
             without the lion?
             I doesn't seem so to me, since he

PEDRO
DE
ARAGON

would in all things, altogether, be
against the French.
If his affairs are easy.
And since it's said the most honest man will win,
that's reason for them all to expect to lose,
every last one.
But know that, in any case,
I'm keeping Castelbon.

*

The
Count
of
Foix

The French, who in the world have none
their peers for greatness of heart and
knowledge of force,
with the Burgundians, will lead to Rome
the Catharists and him who has
himself called king of Aragon.
And to the conflagration will be
led, those who have sinned,
as a matter of consequence and reason,
and one and all burned, their
ashes thrown to the wind.
And to assuage your sorrow,
they'll have such end as surf makes of sand,
and'll know with tears and terror their damnation.

We shall see
vultures walking on the earth,
and such rain as no season can let fall.
And we shall see their lord girt
about, and hung like a thief.
This joglar who cries pardon, yet
only denies our creed,
it won't take longer than a month, I say,
they'll crush his nuts to have the seed.
Then we'll see each one of his opinion
and of his house, dying off in prison.

GIRAUT RIQUIER

(c. 1254—1282)

No existing vida. See notes.

Ab plazen / pessamen

With a pleasant
heaviness,
amorous,
I've smarting
burning pain,
evil desires,
turbulent head,
wherefore nights I cannot sleep
I toss and whip around in bed
and want to see
the dawn.

Now this parcel
of affliction
nags at me
night and day,
I'm lacking joy.
So with gloomy
heart, I'm slacking
off, can't care.
Evening doubles my crucifixion
for on her's all my reflection.
Then how I want
to see dawn!

Her displeasure
makes long evenings,
lying sleepless
without pleasure,
bedding down
but not to rest.
Sour, without profit or joy,
the nights I lie awake and sigh,
restless when
dawn doesn't come.

To my hurt
it would seem
night's too long.
Bitterness?
I've too much,
and distress
that she doesn't match my love.
All night I worry to find ease
when all I want to see
's the dawn.

ANONYMOUS

Mort m'an li semblan que madona·m fai
  E li seu bel oil amoros e gai

The intimations kill me
that my lady gives me
when her handsome eyes
are bright and full of love.

If I fail the closeness
and have no part of her
the intimations kill me / that my lady gives me
I shall go before her
hands folded like a beggar
the intimations kill me / that my lady gives me
to request that she
make consolation for me,
a soft kiss at least.
The intimations kill me / that my lady gives me
when her handsome eyes / are bright and full of love.

Her body's white as snow is
fallen upon ice
the intimations kill me / that my lady gives me
and her color is so fresh
as, in May, a rose
the intimations kill me / that my lady gives me.
Above her face the ashen gold
of hair that pleases me
is softer and more lovely
than my words can say.
The intimations kill me / that my lady gives me
when her handsome eyes / are bright and full of love.

God has made no other
as beautiful as she is
the intimations kill me / that my lady gives me
nor will make another

and besides I love her
the intimations kill me / that my lady gives me
I love her for her straight and slender
body while I live,
and I shall die, believe it,
if I cannot have her love.

The intimations kill me
that my lady gives me
when her handsome eyes
are bright and full of love.

A l'entrada del tens clar

With the coming of clear days
           Aia!
to stir up the gayeties
           Aia!
and float the gilos, damn his eyes
           Aia!
our queen wants to show us how
she can be amorous .

           On your way, on your way, jalous
           Let us now, now let us
           dance among ourselves, 'mong
              ourselves, US.

She's had it posted everywhere that
           Aia!
from here to the sea, may not be
           Aia!
any virgin, lass or laddie,
           AIA!
who doesn't come to swing his chance
in the dancing, joyous.

           On your way, on your way, jalous
           Let us now, now let us
           dance among ourselves, 'mong
              ourselves, US.

The king comes along from elsewhere
           Aia!
to break up the dancing here
           Aia!
For he is in fear's grip
           Aia!

that someone will want to strip off
the queen's April-dress.

> On your way, on your way, jalous
> Let us now, now let us
> dance among ourselves, 'mong
> ourselves, US.

But for nothing let him ask
Aia!
for an old man's not her taste
Aia!
but a slender bachelor
Aia!
who'll know how to make her purr,
this appetizing lady!

> On your way, on your way, jalous
> Let us now, now let us
> dance among ourselves, 'mong
> ourselves, US.

Whoever sees her sport dancing
Aia!
her body swaying starboard, port
Aia!
will say, surely without trouble
Aia!
that the world has not her double
April Queens are joyous!

> On your way, on your way, jalous
> Let us now, now let us
> dance among ourselves, 'mong
> ourselves, US!

Coindeta sui

Got a lover, tell you that
                    pretty? sure I am
Built petite and young and sweet
                    pretty? sure I am
Should have a man who'd make me glad
laughing and playful, not sad
          I'm pretty and in heavy thought
          Got a husband I don't want .

The devil if I ever want him!
                    pretty? sure I am
of if I'm ever loving to him
                    pretty? sure I am
I look at him, don't care a damn, wish
he'd drop dead, can't stand that man!
          I'm pretty and in heavy thought
          Got a husband I don't want .

Just one thing where I'll agree
                    pretty? sure I am
my lover'll make it up to me
                    pretty? sure I am
Waiting for him, right now
wonder why he takes so long
          I'm pretty and in heavy thought
          Got a husband I don't want .

Now we'll get to end this song
                    pretty? sure I am
My lover's loved me for so long
                    pretty? sure I am
my loving body's ready to
prove the thing we want to do
          I'm pretty and in heavy thought
          Got a husband I don't want .

ANONYMOUS

Into this tune the words are bound
                     pretty? sure I am
Let it be sung for miles around
                     pretty? sure I am
Let ladies who have an equal haste
now sing the lover I can taste!
                Pretty? sure I am . Not
                just pretty but in heavy thought,
                got a husband I don't want .

Quan vei los praz verdezir

When I see the meadows greening
and the pomegranate flowers
   then I think with heart and sense
   on love, that's taken residence
   in me and hurt me beyond mending.
   I too often sigh . . .
No lady ever lived so over-
powered and no blow descending. Ai!

All night long I think and sigh,
even in my sleep I shake,
   for it seems to me I feel
   near me, my friend wake.
   God! how quickly I would heal
if he'd make it lightly-
clothed some night in here
and come and steal . . .

The lady who makes move toward love
should hold fine thought within her mind.
   Some madman may lay hold of her
   already thinking of going off.
   I hold my friend with a heart more fine
more loyal, thank heaven,
than any lady of my rank,
more gently given.

That lady who has no lover now
should look for one. For love checks
   us off tomorrow and today
   without any rest or stay.
   Without stroke he wounds and kills,
and cure the sorrow?
nothing serves as remedy
if love's not given.

269

Messenger, rise early, go,
to my friend in his own land
        bring this song. Tell him that
        it much pleased me, words and tune,
        the one he sang after he kissed me
under my pavillion.

In my curtained chamber, he
        moved like a thief!
In my gold-edged chamber
        he was made captive.

Balada cointa e gaia

I'll make a tune for dancing, gay and
pleasant, whoever likes or doesn't.
I'd hear a satisfying music
if I heard you softly groan
night till morning . . .

when my husband's not at home

bel ami

come down here to me

Lover, if I had you here
in my chamber, near me, near—
o, for joy I'd kiss and sigh
for we'd see
dawn next day

when my husband's not at home

bel ami

come down here to me

If the jelos threatens me
with a stick or staff or club,
even if he really drubs me
you've my word
heart won't swerve

when my husband's not at home

bel ami

come down here to me!

NOTES

GUILLEM IX, DUKE OF AQUITAINE

VIDA

Guillem, VII count of Poitou, IX duke of Aquitaine, the first troubadour of record. He succeeded his father, Guilhem VI, in 1086, and so at the age of fifteen came into control of lands more extensive than those of the king of France. Almost 60 years later, with his granddaughter's second marriage, these lands were to form the southern base of the Plantagenet empire.

His wife, Phillipa, was the sole daughter of Guillem IV count of Toulouse. It was his son, Guilhem X, called le Toulousain who fathered this duchess of Aquitaine, but I do not find anywhere that her mother was the duchess of Normandy.

When our Guillem returned from his disastrous crusade early in the 12th C., he found Phillipa absorbed with some religious revival. Not being in much of a mood for spiritual restoratives, he abandoned Phillipa and, according to William of Malmesbury, made off with the countess of Châtellerault. By her previous marriage, the new countess had had a daughter, Anor. It was this girl the old troubadour married to his own heir, and the first-born of this union was named Alianor, who was to be duchess of

Aquitaine, countess of Poitou, queen of France in her first marriage, and queen of England in her second to Henry, duke of Normany, not yet Henry II of England. By this marriage she was to be mother of the young King Henry, Richard Coeur de Lion, Geoffrey of Brittany, and the completely disastrous John Lackland who would oversee the end of the Angevin empire.

Companho, faray un vers . . . covinen

mesclatz : the word is preserved in modern Spanish (mesclado), and in modern Catalan and Mallorquin (mesclat), as well as the contemporary dialects of Occitan. Translated within the line.

Cofolens : confluentum (lat.) to Confluente or Co(n)folens (vulg. lat.), also Conflans, Couflans, Couffoulens, also Coblentz which happens in High-German, that *f* to *b*. Here, Confolens (Charente)

Gimel (Corrèze) arrondissement of Tulle.

Nieul (Charente).

The metric of the third line of each stanza of this and the other two *companho* pieces is interesting. The ancestry of the rhythm begins its known life as the marching tune of Caesar's legions: *Ecce Caesar nunc triumphat qui subegit Gallias*. Hilarius borrowed it for the Church Militant, and it reached Ireland where the legions had never been and became the basis of most Irish meters. The trochaic tetrameter of the *Pervigilium Veneris: Amnis ibat inter arva valle fusus frigida.* It belongs to the African school of the 4th C. In the 9th C. it is a wild *planh* for the slaughter at Fontenay. At the end of the 10th, a wandering scholar sang it in the Rhine valley. After Guillem had used it in his after-dinner entertainments, it turns up as a chamber melody in Venice, and returns to the armed forces on the road to Mandalay, "where the dawn comes up like thunder / out of China 'cross the Bay."

Companho, tant ai agutz d'avols conres

con : (occurring in lines 8, 10, and 12 of the original) cunt. Excuse me. Derived from the same source as our word cuneiform, and from antiquity back into silence. Guillem and Marcabru at least did not boggle at using it and other words at a similar level of the vocabulary. If it was good enough for the 9th duke of Aquitaine, it's good enough for you. I figure these people 800-odd years ago were having a good time, or a bad time, and why shouldn't you know about it?

Farai un vers de dreyt nien

No commentator seems to have pointed out what seems to me quite explicit about this piece: that it is a highly efficient satire on the commonplaces of the whole body of Occitan lyric. Guillem is the first troubadour of whose work we have any record, and died in 1127. He is already bored with the poses of being fated, of being sorcered, of being so dizzy from love that the troubadour cannot tell if he's coming or going or asleep or awake, of being sick and near death from the lady's refusals—even the theme of "the love afar" is there, which we do not otherwise find until Jaufre Rudel sings the countess of Tripoli in the *middle* of the 12th C.

This is only to point up that such a tradition existed, sufficiently advanced to have developed its clichés by the time the piece was composed, perhaps as early as the end of the 11th C.

Farai un vers pos mi sonelh

EN Gari(n) : *en* is the equivalent of the English title "Sir," and is the accented syllable of the full title *senher,* which can be translated equally well as "Lord."

St. Leonart : patron of criminals and other prisoners, especially honored in Auvergne and the Limousin. The hills were full of bandits.

Ned : *Mo net,* my nephew; Ned is the English reduction. This tornada is not included at all in the Hill & Bergin *Anthology,* nor in Jeanroy's critical edition, except in the long footnote where it is labeled apocryphal. The footnote however gives the complete texts of mss. N and C. Through an incomplete reading of the notes in the critical edition, I came across the tornada first in the ms. BN 856 (that's *C*) in the Bibliothèque Nationale in Paris, leaf 232 recto and verso; the *Mo net* strophe is on the *vo.*

> Mo net, tu miras al mati
> Mo vers portaras e·l borssi
> Dreg a la molher d'en Gari

e d'en Bernat;
E diguas lor que per m'amor,
aucizo·l gat.

[E: The *tornada* (also called *envoi*) is a way in which many troubadour lyrics conclude. It is apostrophic in that the poet addresses a messenger, his joglar/jongleur, or his beloved—the latter under a disguised name known as a *senhal* (lit. signal or sign). Blackburn identifies it here and elsewhere explicitly but also expects his readers to do so for themselves hereafter.]

The story the vers tells is itself interesting; my guess is that it's Arabic in origin. Guillem spent much of his youth at the court of Aragon, and the opulence of that court was chiefly Moorish. When Sancho-Ramirez of Aragon was killed before Huesca in 1094, Guillem married Phillipa, the king's young widow. He had to go fetch her and spent perhaps the summer and autumn of that year in Spain.

With Alfons I of Aragon, he participated in a raid into Andalusia in 1115, around Córdoba, and as far south as Grenada, bringing thousands of mozarabe families back to Aragon as prisoners.

According to Orderic Vital, Guillem was captured by the Saracens late in the First Crusade. All this, in addition to the metric evidences—who can say that he did not know Arabic or hadn't heard their songs and stories, if not in Spain in the early years, then in Palestine?

Ben vuelh que sapchon li pluzor

"But/give me a tenso on love..." : *juec d'amor* (game of love) has another quite obvious meaning, necessitating also two players, though the term is a normal one for a tenso. [E: a *tenso* is a poem in the form of a debate.] I chose to translate only the formalized side of the double-meaning chiefly because the reference is an historical one and proves that the tenso form existed prior to any recorded instance of it. The first tenso we have is Cercamon's with Guilhalmi, which can be placed in April or May of 1137.

With *juec d'amor* followed and backed by the verb *triar*, a dicing term as late as the 18th C., we would say perhaps "bracketed" (3 dice), the pun would reach neat but I think untranslatable proportions. If two dice in the game were to be represented by the lady's thighs, and the third by the man's... well, you see what I mean. This is strengthened by the tentatively suggested etymology in my Dauzat: from the Vulgar Latin *tritare*, meaning to crush between millstones or something like that. My translation "to choose" gives the sense, but not the meaning.

St. Julian : the Hospitaller, patron of travelers. The joke is self-explanatory.

Pus vezem de novelh florir

Who he is at Narbonne I do not know. I translate *Esteve* as "my old Bagpipe" because this last stanza seems addressed to a joglar, and an *esteva* was some kind of wind instrument, probably a sort of bagpipe.

Pos de chantar m'es pres talentz

The reference to Folque d'Anjou allows us to fix an approximate date for the poem: 1110-12 or perhaps 1117.

Raymond de St. Gilles, the count of Toulouse, left for the Holy Land on the 1st crusade toward the end of October 1096. Claiming the rights of his wife, Phillipa, daughter of Guillem IV of Toulouse, our Guillem invaded the Toulousain while Raymond was fighting in Palestine. Guillem took the city of Toulouse in July 1098. His first son, referred to here, was born in 1099 in that city, and was stigmatized ever afterward as Guillem the Toulousain.

Several times during our troubadour's life, he had been under papal excommunication for monastery-raiding and other infractions of the Church's rights; also on morals charges, which is understandable. While he held the power in Toulouse, it is highly likely that he was threatened again with—what did they call it?—the thunderbolt of anathema. In any case, we see him leaving the town and himself going on crusade in 1101.

It was thought that this piece was a crusade song, and following that tradition, I so marked it myself in *Proensa* in 1952. But in 1101 his son would have been only two years old, and Folque only nine or eleven (having been born in 1090 or 1092, making the composition of the song at that date highly improbable.

Diez suggests that the piece was composed on the occasion of a pilgrimage, and sets the date not before 1110-12. Guillem IX would have been 39 or 41, his son 11 or 13, and Folque d'Anjou 18, 20, or 22 years old.

Jeanroy puts the date at 1117, the year his last communication was lifted. In this case, Guillem would have been 46, his son 18, and Folque 25 or 27. Either of these last two is a reasonable guess.

seisin : legal term meaning possession of lands or chattel. The man who granted it would have been the king of France, whose vassal the count of Poitou was, nominally.

CERCAMON

Car vei finir a tot dia

[E: Guilhalmi is the same poet (possibly a jongleur) mentioned above in Blackburn's note on Guillem de Poitou's *Ben vuelh que sapchon li pluzor.*]

The background of this tenso is the then-imminent marriage of Eleanor of Aquitaine to the future Louis VII of France. Guillem X, Eleanor's father, had died April 9, 1137, and the marriage date had first been fixed for May 30 of that year, though the wedding did not finally take place until July. The count of Poitou who is coming is, of course, young Louis. This would date the tenso between April 9 and the end of May.

Ab lo temps qe fai refrescar

In the tornada of this piece is the first mention of that advanced stage of the *drudaria;* the lover sees his lady alone and without clothing between them.

EDITOR'S NOTE

Per fin' amor m'esjauzira

This poem is of doubtful attribution.

MARCABRU

VIDA I

Panperdut one might translate literally as "Lostbread." Or more contemporarily as "fuckup." He certainly lost a lot of bread singing his major theme since the social level under fire would have represented his major way of earning a living. Even though Marcabru was apparently recognized as a major figure, he was naturally an embarrassing presence in more elegant courts. Despite his tavern language, and perhaps that was where he had to end up singing finally, it is the loss of the earlier, more noble tradition he complains of. He is very much a moralist (as you will hear).

"In those days no one called them cansos...." An incredible amount of Occitan scholarship, commentary and lectures, depends upon this sentence. When the scribe in the second vida uses the term *sirventes*, he is using his contemporary term to describe (accurately) what did not yet exist as form toward the early middle of the 12th century.

"...and listened to throughout the world...." After having rambled through Poitou and the southwest, he seems to have crossed the Pyrenees into Spain and become a soldier against the Saracens (1138-42). From references within the body of his work [E: about 42 extant pieces], he appears to have traveled also in the north of France and perhaps in England.

EDITOR'S NOTES

Aujatz de chan com enans' e meillura

The second line of the second stanza of the translation echoes Dante's *Inferno* III. 56-57, an example of enrichment by anachronism, though from our perspective the proximity of Dante's and Marcabru's lifetimes diminishes the anachronistic effect.

The Count of Poitou refers to William (Guillem) X of Aquitaine, the son of Guillem IX, the troubadour. The "other Amfos over near León" refers to Alfonso VII of Castille and León, who was also one of Marcabru's patrons.

L'autrier jost' un sebissa

The pastorela is a type of poem in which the poet or his persona relates an attempt (usually unsuccessful) to seduce a peasant girl.

Estornel, cueill ta volada

Elias refers to the prophet Elijah.

St. Privat is an obscene pun—seen and pointed out by most editors.

Al departir del brau tempier

Berard de Monleydier was regarded as a "model of courtesy and success in love, known...from Bodel's *Chanson des Saisnes*" (Bergin and Hill, II.

38). At least two other troubadours refer to Berard for his gallantry, Bertran de Born in *Volontiers feira sirventes* (Bergin and Hill, I. 111), which Blackburn did not translate, and Peire Vidal in *Drogoman, senher, s'agues bon destrier*, for which see below, p. 114.

"LAUDATOR . TEMPORIS . ACTI" is Blackburn's own addition, following Dejeanne's note on the poem: "Comme le precedent [*A l'alena de vent doussa*], c'est un chant de printemps et un sirventes. Marcabru est *laudator temporis acti*" (*Poésies complètes du troubadour Marcabru*, Toulouse, 1909, p. 216). For the source of this appellation for praisers of the past, see Horace, *Ars Poetica*, vs. 173.

Per savi'l tenc ses doptansa

"For Love has the sign/of emerald and sard": According to the medieval lapidary, the emerald discourages lust while the sard encourages chastity, humility, and restraint.

L'iverns vai e'l temps s'aizina

Sir Eglain most likely does not refer to anybody historical.

Sir Ebles refers to Ebles II of Ventadorn, a contemporary and rival of Guillem IX. None of Ebles' poems have survived. Bernard de Ventadorn also attacked Ebles' poetry and theory of love as irrational.

Dirai vos en mon lati

Sir Constans is Blackburn's translation of *Costans*, "a proper noun" that "stands for the talebearers and the false lovers in Marcabru's songs" (Frederick Goldin, *Lyrics of the Troubadours and Trouvères*, p. 85).

JAUFRÉ RUDEL

Quan lo rius de la fontana

The tornada or envoi to this piece is addressed to Uc VII of Lusignan, who had taken the Cross for the 2nd Crusade in 1147.

[E: Filhol is the name of the joglar.]

BERNART DE VENTADORN

The general inaccuracy of the vidas and razos might best be pointed out here. Referred to as the duchess of Normandy (not countess of Poitou or duchess of Aquitaine, which areas comprised her dowry), Eleanor was already married to Henry duke of Normandy and count of Anjou on May 18, 1152, scarcely eight weeks after the decree of Beaugency (March 21), an august conclave which passed and announced her separation from Louis VII of France. The Plantagenet duke was a lusty 18, and Eleanor was pushing 30. In the fall of 1152, the newly married couple made a progress through her southern provinces, Poitou and the Limousin. This would have been a likely time for Bernart, now at loose ends after the brouhaha at Ventadour, to have joined their court. Henry Plantagenet was away in England on politics and war from January 1153 until the spring of 1154. This would have provided more than ample time for an affair between the young duchess and the poet.

It was the Sunday before Christmas, 1154, that Henry and Eleanor were crowned in Westminster Abbey, London.

Even the statement in the final paragraph, definite as it sounds, is suspect. We know that Ebles IV, son of the viscountess of Ventadour, was already married in 1174, while Uc de St. Circ seems to have been born only toward the end of the 12th C., and is certainly the author of the vida for Savaric de Mauléon, if not this one. Appel questions the value of the evidence in any case, of Ebles IV, or at worst Ebles V, fifty years after the events had taken place.

The razo is even more circumstantial, and in this case, downright botched. For a fuller version of the same story, see the razo marked III under Raimbaut de Vaqueiras. I include this version here purely to indicate the amount of confusion and inaccuracy the scribes were capable of perpetuating. Should someone trace the story of the "other man's cloak" back to some Arabic tale, I wouldn't be a bit surprised. That it occurs more than once in different contexts points to the possibility of there being a common source.

BEATRITZ DE DIA

VIDA

The identity of this earliest of the *trobairitz* (lady troubadours—certainly as awful a term as "poetesses"), is by no means sure. Pillet thinks she is Beatrix, daughter of Guillen II of Poitou, comte de Valentinois. Jeanroy discusses the difficulty of identifying her husband, and further suggests that Raimbaut d'Aurenga is not the troubadour of that name, but a nephew of his who lived in the first half of the 13th C. One of her five surviving pieces is a tenso with this Raimbaut, or the Raimbaut. Her poetry is simple, direct, and sincere by comparison.

EDITOR'S NOTE

Estat ai en greu cossirier

Floris and Blancheflor were the hero and heroine of a popular medieval romance entitled after them.

PEIRE D'ALVERNHE

Chantarai d'aquestz trobadors

Though d'Alvernhe calls this a *vers*, I call it a *sirventes:* it's about time to introduce the term. The *canso*, as a term for the love lyric, entered with de Ventadorn's *Can vei* as far as this collection is concerned, although at least two of Guillem de Peitau's, Cercamon's *Ab lo temps*, and both of Jaufré Rudel's pieces might be defined as cansos in terms of their subject matter. So also, Marcabru's tavern-language critiques of the nobility, especially of the ladies, might be called sirventes. A sirventes could be concerned with anything but love: social criticism, politics, personal satire, social satire, downright sermonizing, any combination of subject, as long as it was not a love song and the singer was bugged about something. It seems that it was not necessary to compose a fresh melody for such pieces, and any known

NOTES TO PAGE 85

tune could be used. In this case, the tune literally "served" the words, which may be the origin of the term "sirventes." In one of the vidas of Bertran de Born it is reported that the king of Aragon was of the opinion that "the tunes of Giraut de Bornelh made good wives for de Born's sirventes." For a discussion of the technical differences between the vers and the canso, see Aimeric de Peguilhan's *Mantas vetz*, p. 203.

In the vida, I translate *la bona gen* as the Catharists. These heretics (called more commonly "the Albigensians" for no known reason, since their stronghold was Toulouse which has always been a more important town than Albi) were known throughout the south as "the good men," *les bonhommes*. I cannot otherwise see the point of mentioning that our poet "did penance and died." I suspect the term is still in widespread use throughout the south in its weakened meaning, i.e., without the old religious overtones. In Toulouse at least it is still used to designate almost any poor worker or common man: "Ah, voui, j'en ai parlé avec un bonhomme à la gare." Say about the luggage and why it hasn't arrived.

Cobla, literally a "couplet," is here taken to mean strophe.

Pound has made the reasonable surmise that Giraut de Bornelh's fine reputation during his own time may have been based on the attractiveness of his tunes (see the quote from the king of Aragon *supra*). I have included no piece of Giraut's. Pound translated the alba, *Reis glorios, verais lums e clartatz*—no need to repeat a good job—and I did not read through his entire *chansonnier* (80 pieces), but I found him generally dull, windy, and a master of the cliché. No piece of his I tried would turn into anything resembling an interesting poem in English. Let his reputation rest on Pound's version of the *Reis glorios:* it's better than he deserves.

The Limousin from Brive (go there sometime: the medieval center of that town has a melancholy beauty that is most affecting, and there's the bridge too, over the Corrèze before it meets the Vezère), might be Uc de Bacalaria (*joglars fo de pauca valor*) "he was a joglar of little valor, traveled little, and was little known," for his vida mentions only that he was from the Limousin. But although he did "make good cansos, made one good descort and good tensos," the simplest joglar would be likely to have a good voice, given his trade. My own guess is that the man referred to is Gaucelm Faidit. His birthplace is given as Uzerche. That's just south of Brive, and his vida states that *cantava peiz d'ome del mon*, i.e., he sang worse than any man in the world. That fits.

The phrase "two aspirin" in the Guillem de Ribas stanza has been criticized as a glaring anachronism. The original reads: *e l'uelh semblan de vout d'argen*, i.e., his eyes look like silver statuettes. I think the feeling of dullness is translated.

En Raimbautz (#9) is surely Raimbaut d'Aurenga, perhaps the sometime lover of the countess of Poitou (see p. 282).

The "ancient Lombard" is Bertran de Born: medieval equivalent to calling him an old Jew. See de Born's *Be·m platz*, "Pawn your castles, lords." Both Jews and Lombards had reputations as moneylenders. There is still a Lombard Street in London and it still has pawnshops in it. The "bastard words" : *marabotz* is an adjectival form. A marabotin was an ancient Spanish coin, also the metal used in the coin, probably with the connotation of "alloy" derived from the Arabic *marâbitî*.

There is an alternate stanza describing the troubadour himself: one can reasonably assume that it was not by his own hand.

> Peire d'Alvernhe a tal votz
> que canta cum granolh' em potz,
> e lauza·s mout a tota gen;
> pero maistres es de totz
> ab q'un pauc es clarzis ses motz,
> qu'a penas nulhs hom los enten.

which goes roughly:

> Peire d'Alvernhe has such a voice that
> he sings like a frog in a cesspool,
> and praises himself rather too much
>   to all men.
> But he is master of all, provided
> he clarify his words a bit, for
> hardly anyone understands them.

[E: For further information on the identities of the troubadours named in this poem, see Bergin and Hill, II. 26-28.]

ARNAUT DE MAREUIL

VIDA

Mareuil (Dorgogne): I use the modern French spelling to normalize the place name. In the manuscripts you'll find Maroill, Maruoill, Marueill, Maruelh, Marvoill, Merueil, Meruoill, Miroill, and Miroilh. Some of these may be simply copyists' mistakes, but they also reflect slight differences in pronunciation from area to area. (It would take a better linguist than I to demonstrate that scientifically.) The name means "the big clearing," and is derived from the gallic *Maroialos*. Gallic words are not necessarilly celtic; they seem to have borrowed a number of words and radicals from their predecessors, especially the Ligurians.

The point I would make here is that neither the pronunciation nor the orthography was particularly standardized. Especially in the poems, I use the version that suits my ear at that point. In the razo here I use Anfos for the king of Aragon: the name is also Amfos, Alfons—I don't remember using the French Alphonse ever. Let no prospective student of occitan be put off by the spelling variants in different editions, anthologies, chrestomathies, etc. It doesn't matter whether the angry husband is called the *gilos* or the *jelos,* as long as he is recognized for what he is.

Countess of Burlatz: Azalais of Toulouse, daughter of the count Raimon V (1184-1194): brought up apparently in the castle of Burlatz (canton of Roquecourbe, in the arrondissement of Castres, Tarn). In 1171 she married Roger II, viscount of Béziers and Carcassonne, who was called Talliafero (or Taillefer, or Eisenhower, iron-cutter, or however you want to translate that).

"mother of the viscount whom the French murdered, etc." Raimon-Roger, born in 1185, succeeded his father in 1194. In the summer of 1209 he was defending Carcassonne against the crusading army. It was a hot summer and the wells were drying up. When the papal legate, Arnauld de Citeaux, invited the young viscount to discuss terms of capitulation, he accepted and was detained as a prisoner. This treachery ended the siege, and of those who had not fled, 50 were hanged and 400 burnt alive. The town was pillaged but not burnt; the interests of the crusading army had to be considered. But the legates apologized to Innocent III for not having duplicated the holocaust of Béziers. The viscount was imprisoned in a dungeon in his own castle, was perhaps murdered, in any case died shortly thereafter, age 24.

King Anfos: Alfons II of Aragon (died 1196). If one can believe a sirventes of Guillem de Berguedan addressed to Alfons, he was not particularly grateful to Azalais:

> The countess who is lady of Béziers,
> you took from her, when she gave you love,
> two cities and a hundred castles with towers.

Guillen de Montpellier : Guillem VIII (died in 1202). Guillem's court at Montpellier with his wife, Eudoxia of Constantinople, was well known for its hospitality to singers.

The evidence in both cansos of the steps involved in the troubadour's courtship of the married woman is interesting. After private conversations between the lady and the poet were acceptable, the first sign of admission as an established suitor was the giving of a kiss. The next step in the direction of intimacy seems to have been that the lover was permitted to watch his lady preparing for bed, and to see her very lightly clothed or naked—and to adore. The presumably final step was to have the privilege of spending the whole night next to her naked. The final carnal knowledge was supposed to have been avoided, for the usual religious and legal reasons, but also for aesthetic ones. "Fine love" was where that final knowledge was not shared; this *amor pur* stopping short of the fact itself was the most highly prized and honored, since all other intimacies were permitted, kisses, caresses, and the possibility, and God knows, the temptation to carry matters to the next lower category, "mixed love." (See Marcabru for some hard words on the subject.) This slow increase in intimacy—one gets the impression that it took years to reach the final stages—must have produced incredible ecstacies on both parties to such a love, turning the joys of the flesh into something as close to spiritual ecstacy as any religion could produce. That such a process would also push the lovers to an incredible point of impatience, the woman as well as the man, doubtless turned many a pure love into a mixed one.

The last stanza in *Bel m'es quan lo vens m'alena*, while acknowledging the stages of the troubadour's courting, goes directly to a very clear description of the sexual act. In the fifth stanza of *Bel m'es lo dous temps amoros*, the use of the word *solace* is quite specific, as well as the reference to the undressing. The mention of "hands' games" in that context makes one speculate, not very hard, as to what specific caresses one could expect in the final stage of *amor pur*. The practical view is that one settled for what one could get.

Though more sincerely lyrical than many singers, Arnaut's pieces seem solidly based in the prospect of carnal satisfactions, and he does not seem very discreet in his propositions. Maybe he had better luck that way.

ARNAUT DANIEL

VIDA

Ribeyrac is near Périgord in the Dordogne. The castle was situated on a high point commanding the left bank of the Dronne. It had been built around 920-940 A.D., and was the seat of a viscount in Arnaut's day.

The lady of Buovilla is something of a mystery; even the location of the town is. There are several it might be, but none of them in the Gascoigne. Miguel de la Tor says that Arnaut loved a Gascon lady from Agrismonte, which opens up another three or four towns, two of them in Catalonia. I don't think it matters too much. There was a Guillem de Bouvila who was an armed knight of Raimon VII of Toulouse in 1244 . . . o well.

The four quoted lines are the tornada to the canso given here. This piece was apparently the most popular of any of Arnaut's pieces during his own time and for a couple of centuries after, presumably because of the very striking metaphor in the second line. Peire d'Alvernhe's sirventes on his fellow singers does not mention Arnaut; it was composed between 1170 and 1180. But the Monk of Montaudon's sirventes on the same subject, composed between 1190 and 1200, refers directly to this piece, contrasting it to Daniel's reputation as an exponent of *trobar clus*. In Pound's collection of Daniel he leaves out *En cest sonet*, not finding it technically interesting enough. Read his versions for a sense of the texture of the originals brought over into English. It may seem a shame to represent one of the greatest technicians of all time by this one piece, but it's useless to do a good job twice. The Trucs Malecs sirventes I omit, though I've made a good version of it, for the same reasons as E.P.—it's pretty dirty.

RAZO

"...at the court of king Richard of England.": this would have been in Poitiers, the seat of the counts of Poitou and dukes of Aquitaine (today the *palais de justice*). The time could have been either between 1189 and 1191, before the crusade, or between 1194-1199 after Richard's return from captivity. Over his ten years as king of England, Coeur de Lion spent only very brief periods in that country.

En cest sonet coind' e leri :

Lusena: (or Luserna) Canello eliminates the Lucerne in Switzerland and Luserna-San-Giovanni in the Piedmont SW of Turin: he connects the lady with an Aragonese, and the town, mentioned in another poem, with Lucena, NW of Castellon in the province of Valencia.

"I do not want the Roman Emp. / nor to be elected pope" : Canello notes that in 1191, and again in 1216, both the imperial throne and the papacy had vacancy signs out. The earlier date more likely?

"than Mondis loved Audierna" : (Monclis?) The reference has proved unidentifiable. It seems likely that they were lovers known from some epic or popular legend which we've lost.

PEIRE VIDAL

VIDA and RAZOS

Saint Gilles (Gard).

Alazais de Rocamartina (Roquemartine, the ruins thereof, is NW of Aix, about halfway toward Avignon) of the Porcellet family, was the first wife of Raimon Gaufridi Barral, viscount of Marseille, who put her aside some time before 1191; he died himself in 1192. Alazais (or Azalais, Fr. Adélaide) lived in the vicinity of Arles until 1201 (Stronski).

". . . until he went overseas with King Richard" : no secondary sources to substantiate this, though there are sympathetic references to Coeur de Lion in *A per pauc de chantar no·m lais,* written while Richard was captive of the Hohenstaufen Roman Emperor Henry VI (1193-94), and after his release in *Ben viu a gran dolor.* In 1201 or 1202 Peire composed a crusade song, *Baros Jesus qu'en crotz fo fes,* and was evidently on Malta in 1204 or 1205 (*Neus ni gels ni ploja ni fanh*). This latter would have been the 4th crusade, that disgrace, not the 3rd in which Richard was central.

March 25, 1199, at the siege of Châlus, Richard caught a shaft from a strongbow in the shoulder below the nape and near his spine. When the garrison of Châlus had surrendered, Richard interviewed his slayer, pardoned him, and died on the 6th of April. The head of the arrow had gone so deep it could not be removed.

Les Baux : near Arles and Tarascon—some of the most impressive ruins in Provence.

"in grief over the death of the good count . . ." : Raimon V of Toulouse, d. 1194. The long list of Catalan and Aragonese knights who accompanied Alfons suggests that the biographer might have been Catalan.

La Loba : from one of the razos on Raimon de Miraval, another of the several troubadours who sang this lady:

But he loved a lady of Carcassonne who was
called Loba de Puenautier, the daughter of
en Raimon de Puegnautier, and who was married
to a rich and powerful knight of Le Cabardès . . .
(follows a description of the lady) and all
the valorous men and noble barons of the area
who met her fell in love with her: the count
of Foix, en Oliviers de Saissac, en Peire
Rotgiers de Mirepoix, en Aimeric de Montréal,
and en Peire Vidal who made many good cansos
for her.

Ma domna Estefania : the wife of Bernart d'Alion, the lord of Son (the castle of Donezan near Foix, Ariège, in the Basses-Pyrénées). She is referred to by the senhal Bels-Sembelis in *Ges pel temps fer e brau* and *De chantar m'ora laissatz*, neither of which is in this selection from Vidal's fifty-odd pieces. The standard edition is Joseph Anglade's.

Ma domna Raimbauda de Biolh : (Alpes-Maritimes). Peire Vidal sings this lady in *Tart mi veiran mei amic en Tolosa* and again in *De chantar m'era laissatz.* "The ladies of Biolh" show up in what seems to be a much earlier piece: *En una terra estranha:*

> God keep the ladies of Biolh
> for, in them are worth and valor,
> joy, solace, and love, all beauty
>   and all pleasure, all
> of lovely intelligence and knowing.
> When God sees all the virtues in them
> surely he'll place them next him.

"...the king had arms made for himself and for Peire Vidal and had clothes made for both of them..." : see parag. 2 of razo I., where Alazais also presents him with arms "and they dressed alike". These signs of particular intimacy, wherein here evidence that they took place between lover and lady as well as between men-friends, are strikingly parallel to blood-brother rituals. Whole area for investigation of this relationship. The blood-relationship in this sense has always been considered the next important to marriage in intimacy and the specific binding of individuals to one another.

Plus que·l paubres que jatz e·l ric ostal :

The Lord of Excideuil : Richard Coeur de Lion.

Geoffrey : Richard's brother, Geoffrey Plantagenet, count of Brittany.

Bel-Castiat : The identity of most senhals cannot be proved absolutely. But there are likelihoods given various internal evidence in the songs, in the vidas and razos when they are not totally deduced from the songs themselves, and occasional secondary sources such as documents with dates and names and places. Castiat and Vierna are names which appear more often in Vidal's tornadas than any others. For Castiat Bartsch proposes Olivier de Saissac or Aimeric de Montréal; Anglade thinks Raimond V, count of Toulouse (1148-1194) more likely. So do I.

Vierna : it seems very likely that this name designates Alazais de Rocamartina, wife of Barral of Marseille. In *Drogoman senher*, where there are clearly disparaging references to the count of Toulouse, the tornada is addressed to Vierna and Rainier (Barrals). In *Bels amics cars, ven s'en vas vos estius*, where the tornada is dedicated to both Vierna and to Castiat, we can note the separation in space between Peire's two favorite people:

> *Na Vierna, tornar e remaner*
> *Volgra ves vos, si m'en dones lezer*
> *Mos Castiatz, mas trop se fai temer.*

Vierna, I'd want to come back
and be with you if my Castiat
would give me leisure to do so.
Guess he's too afraid I'll stay

The four kings of Spain : the kings of Castille, Aragon, Navarre and Leon; certainly Alfons VIII of Castille (1158-1214) and Alfons IX of Leon (1188-1230); the other two would depend upon a fairly precise dating of the poem. It would seem to be during his exile from Marseille—perhaps he spent part of it traveling through Spain, not just sitting in Genoa as the razo suggests? The references to Richard and Geoffrey seem polite though full of praise, without the feeling of warmth and intimacy that might have been there had they shared the planks of a ship together. Which might date the piece before the 3rd crusade, i.e., prior to the summer of 1190. In that case, it would be Alfons II of Aragon (1162-1196) and Sancho VI of Navarre (1150-1194). Coeur de Lion married Sancho's daughter, Berengaria, the summer of 1190 in Limassol on Cyprus, en route to Palestine. If the piece is later than I think, the monarchs might have been Pedro II of Aragon (1196-1213) and Sancho VII of Navarre (1194-1234).

Anglade says that the latest we can date any poem of Peire's is 1205, so that he may not have lived to see his good advice taken. The kingdom of Leon stayed out of it, but Sancho VII was with Alfons VIII of Castile and Alfons II of Aragon at the battle of Las Navas de Tolosa, July 16, 1212, which broke the back of the Mohammedan power in Spain. Yakub al-Mansur, emir of the Almohades, was the losing pitcher.

Una canso ai faita mortalmen

"the squire who died at table" : No one knows who he was; figure from a romance we've lost?

"May I die accursed in hell..." : Vidal is sometimes thought to have flirted with heresy. It seems unlikely somehow.

Drogoman senher, s'agues bon destrier

[E: a *vanto* is a boasting poem.]

Drogoman, the lord Expositor : Anglade suggests the count of Toulouse; how? The piece seems clearly anti-Toulousain and pro-Aragonese. My vote is for Guillem VIII, marquis de Montpellier and the tornada sends his regards specifically from that city. (G. de Montpellier died in 1202). Another possibility is Sancho, son of the king of Aragon, who governed (held forth?) in his name in Provence (1181-85). Anyway, Peire seems to have been in some trouble at the court of the count of Toulouse, hometown boy makes good, etc.

Sir Guy : Gui de Lusignan, whom he might have met on crusade?

"the king would live serene..." : Alfons II of Aragon; Balaguier is a Catalan town.

Aspe and Ossau are two towns in the Basses-Pyrénées.

Estat ai gran sazo

There were so many good things in this canso that I hated to scrap it because of an equally heavy load of clichés: nor would a simple cutting and re-ordering of the continuity pull it together. A solution appeared when I remembered a number of isolated lines, stanzas, individual images scattered throughout Vidal's whole chansonnier of about 50 pieces, which had pricked my imagination in the reading, but did not seem at the time sufficient motive to undertake the whole piece. I should like to indicate these intercalations and the sources of each. The references are to Anglade's edition.

"From the thicket....soft!"

Two sources: p. 38, XIII, V, 32-35;

> *Plus que l'auzels qu'ès noiritz lai per Fransa,*
> *Quant hom l'apel' et el respon coitos*
> *E sap qu'es mortz, paus mon cor voluntos*
> *Als mils cairels qu'ab sos bels olhs mi lansa.*

and p. 23f, IX, III, 18-19;

> *E son cairel el cor mis*
> *Et anc mais colps tan no·m plac...*

"But I see roses....overcast."

p. 47, XVI, I, 9-10;

> *Paro·m rozas entre gel*
> *E clars temps ab trebol cel.*

And that bird was still with me.

"I have no walled castle....lover."

p. 7, III, IV, 25-28;

> *Non ai castel serrat de mur*
> *Ni ma terra no val dos gans,*
> *Mas anc no fo plus fis amans*
> *De mi...*

Since there will be no second opportunity, I'd like to offer here a few other Peire Vidal passages which got to me—ones I did not interpolate. Two of them gloss the rules and conditions of courtly love; the rest I give solely for their own qualities.

p. 6, III, III, 17-18;

De clartat m'a mes en escur
Cela per cui vauc desirans;

Because of her
I have passed from the clear light into shadow.

p. 7, III, III, 21-24; on waiting to attain that stage where the lover is permitted the intimacy of looking upon his lady naked:

Mas be·us dic que tan sofrirai,
Tro posca en loc avenir,
Qu'ab mos olhs son bel cors remir,
E s'i aura trop al meu par.

But let me tell you how much I'll suffer
before I may come to that place where
I may look upon
with my own eyes
her lovely body
and that as far as I'm concerned, it
will seem too long.

p. 33, XI, VII, 55-57; on the liars and tale-bearers:

Plus que no pot ses aiga viure·l peis,
No pot esser ses lauzengier domneis,
Per qu'amador compron trop car lor joc.

A fish cannot live without water,
nor love at court be without liars,
so lovers buy their joy too dearly.

p. 18, VII, V, 29-30;

Donc car tan l'am, mout sui plus folatura
Que fols pastres qu'a bel poi caramela.

I have gone half-cracked, I have loved her so,
am crazier than
the mad herdsman

294

at his reed
on the soft hillside.

p. 22, VIII, V, 49-53;

Quar plus qu'obra d'aranha
Non pot aver durada
Amors, pos es proada,
Qu'ab ditz daur' et aplanha
Tal qu'a·l cor de vilan escolh:

Love is a spider's web for delicacy,
and will last about as long
if a man be not true.

"Were I next God's throne, lady, and you called . . ." : More food for the heresy charge against Vidal.

"She's been taken by a count . . ." : Loba's lover seems to have been Roger, count of Foix (1188-1223).

"the illustrious marquis and his lovely sister" : Boniface I, marquis of Montferrat. His sister Azalais married Manfred II, marquis of Saluces in 1182.

A per pauc de chantar no·m lais :

The year of this sirventes seems to be 1193. Coeur de Lion (see stanza 4) is still in a German prison; Celestine III is pope; papal legates and missions of preachers and bishops are wandering the south getting decrees passed against the catharists and extorting recantations and public penances from wealthy heretics under the threat of confiscation of their worldly goods; Phillipe-Auguste of France is intriguing with Henry Hohenstaufen, the Holy Roman Emperor to keep the English king prisoner in the fortress chamber at Trifels; and doubtless with the papacy to keep pressure on the good count Raimond of Toulouse, the stronghold of heresy, in return for certain concessions in the Holy Land; Raimond V, meanwhile, is up to his eyebrows in Alfons II's renewal of hostilities with the Toulousain, Aragon having as allies Pere Lara, viscount of Narbonne and Raymond-Roger, count of Foix. Raimon V, Peire Vidal's lord (*Mos Castiatz*), will die this

295

next year, though Richard will be released in February at Mainz when the politicking and the ransoming have ended. But 1193 is a bad year, and no one knows the good news or the bad news of 1194. Things are no better in Spain, with wars between the Christian kings still raging, and many years of retaking Valencia and defeats (Yakub al-Mansur will give Alfonso VIII a good drubbing at Alarcos in La Mancha in July 1195) still ahead.

The last two stanzas to Loba de Pennautier come as something of a relief. What the hell, ro-mance!

RAIMON JORDAN

VIDA I.

Raimon was born around 1150. Sant Antonin is at the confluence of the Aveyron and the Bonnette in the present arrondissement of Montauban. Cahors is just to the north, and both are somewhat north of Toulouse.

Pena d'Alberges (arrondissement de Gaillac, Tarn).

The patarins = catharists = albigensians.

VIDA II.

Elis de Montfort: she doesn't seem to have been Guillem de Gourdon's wife, or at least the historic facts do not seem to work out that way. She was born around 1165 and in 1214 she was married to Bernart de Casnac and lady of Montfort. At least she was not de Gourdon's wife who, around 1165 at Montfort, witnessed a donation of her husband. Might she have been G. de Gourdon's second wife in her first marriage, and B. de Casnac's wife in her second? Does it matter?

The description of the ceremony of receiving a man as knight and lover is interesting and seems like a public ceremony.

Lo clar temps vei brunezir

Set the request in the final stanza, to lie with his lady, against the above.

The statement about God in that stanza, "if I had urgent business with Death" etc., seems to mark the viscount heavily as a heretic himself. These singers keep getting to the real point of the matter, no?

RAIMBAUT DE VAQUEIRAS

VIDA

Vaqueiras, arrondissement d'Orange (Vaucluse). The castle belonged to the prince of Orange who ceded it to the count of Toulouse in 1210.

Peirops : Surprise! "Rocks in the head" is not a neologism.

Guillem des Baux : Guillem IV and his brother Uc (Hugh) were the sons of Bertran de Baux. Their mother, Tiburge, was the sister of Raimbaut, prince of Orange from 1182 until 1219 when he was killed by the people of Avignon. Les Baux (canton de St.-Rémy, arrond. d'Arles) or rather the craggy ruins thereof, was photographed for *Life* magazine about ten years ago.

[E: "Proensa in Stone," *Life*, 35 (July 13, 1953): 76-90.]

Boniface of Montferrat : Jeanroy remarks that R. de Vaqueiras was already "Boniface's man" when he began his relationship with the princes of Les Baux before 1189. Boniface succeeded his father, Guillem III, in 1192. In 1202 he was elected leader of the 4th crusade. He backed Baudoin of Flanders for emperor of Constantinople and received the kingdom of Salonika as thanks. He died in 1207 fighting the Bulgars in the Rhodope Mountains. Jeanroy thinks that Raimbaut first knew Boniface as early as 1175.

Biatritz : Boniface had two sisters, neither one of which was named Beatrice, and neither of which married Enric del Carret. The marquis' daughter, however, *was* named Biatritz, and it is surely she Raimbaut names in at least ten pieces.

Bel Cavalier : Zingarelli makes a strong argument against the senhal designating Beatrice. However, I think the vidas and razos may be accurate here. Many of Raimbaut's pieces carry two tornadas: the first to Beatrice, the second to Bel Cavalier. What better way to hide the true identity of the lady?

RAZO I.

Alazais de Salutz : the marquis' sister who married the marquis of Saluces in 1182 (see the note on Vidal's *Estat ai gran sazo*). Beatrice would have been Alazais' niece, not her sister.

In Beatrice's speech to Raimbaut, madona Alazais is her aunt, and the lady of Marseille Azalais, wife of en Barral. In spite of that *z* shifting around, they are the same name: in English, Adelaide.

RAZO II.

See a garbled version of this tale, I doubt if it's anything more, in the razo for Bernart de Ventadorn's *Can vei*, and the note there on the unreliability of these vidas and razos. It's a nice story, though, isn't it?

"made en Raimbaut a knight" : De Bartholomaeis proposes a date as early as 1195 for the *Tant ai ben dig*. And apropos a tenso between Raimbaut and Albert marquis de Malaspina (Boniface's brother-in-law) dating it about 1194 or 1195, Diez notes that Raimbaut was already a knight before his departure for the crusade (1202). In 1194-95, Raimbaut went with Boniface to the war in Sicily where they fought side by side. Very likely he was knighted for valor in that action. Raimbaut is not heard of after Boniface's death in 1207.

Kalenda maya

estampida : the single example we have of this dance form.

[E: *jelos* is a stock name for the beloved lady's husband. It was spelled variously by medieval scribes—*jalous, gilos*—standardized spelling being a thing of the distant future. Following the practice of the editors in diplomatic editions of the poems, Blackburn retains the different spellings of several words—occasionally of names as well—throughout this work.]

"than Erec did Enida" : Erec and Enida are the hero and heroine of a romance by a French contemporary, Chrétien de Troyes. If you buy the razo, it would make sense. The jongleurs were French and could have recited the romance the night before, that afternoon, etc.

Engles : No one agrees. According to De Bartholomaeis this senhal de-
notes a lady; according to Zingarelli, Boniface. I would agree with Z. But
then in the razo for a piece of Raimbaut's, *Tuit me pregon, Engles, q'eu vos
don saut*, which is all about Guillem des Baux and how he robbed a French
merchant on the road and finally got his comeuppance, had to give it all
back and pay damages, and ended up coming down the Rhône in a boat
borrowed from a fisherman. Then it adds: *En Rambauz de Vaqeiras, qe
s'apelava (ab lui) "Engles" si·n fez aqestas coblas.* I give it up.

[E: Bergin and Hill, II. 57, suggest Boniface.]

Domna, tant ai vos pregada

This false tenso is a joke at the expense of the Genoese dialect at least.
With one stanza in Provençal and the next in Genoese, the elegant courtly
tone of one is contrasted with the harsh vulgarity of the other. The taste of
such a dialect joke is questionable in the original. At first I tried to do the
lady's stanzas in a kind of stage Italian-American, "I'ma goona slitta you
throat" etc., it was too embarrassing, and I settled for a tough New York-
ese tone.

If the satire were directed at an individual, it would clearly have been a
better joke to the 'in' audience. On the other hand, someone in a Provençal
court might have asked: "So! You're just back from Genova. How did you
make out?" And Raimbaut answered: "O, terrible. It was terrible. I had
this tenso, see...?"

I guess I don't think it's very funny, finally. Just the structure: the troubadour goes through the usual courtly compliments with the response that
you see here, friends.

Sir Opetí : Crescini suggests Obizzo II Malaspina, Boniface's brother-in-
law.

BERTRAN DE BORN

VIDAS

Including interpolations of a highly capricious order, these vidas may
serve as models of inaccuracy, half-digested information, seemingly reli-

able apocrypha as to detail, and the exaggeration which must have been perpetrated and maintained by joglars whose livelihood depended on the interest of their audience.

The traditional spiel preceding the performance of any given song or group of songs by a single troubadour was probably remembered in its most striking form, *i.e.*, the most inaccurate one. This would have persisted longest in the oral tradition, and would have been the one the scribe heard who, much later, put it into manuscript.

"and had close to a thousand men" : Very unlikely.

"The king of Aragon said. . . . . sirventes." Aragon's remark is clear if we remember that the sirventes did not require an original tune. It reports, in effect, that de Born used (how many?) of Giraut de Bornelh's melodies as "wives" for his masculine words.

I have not included any of Bornelh's cansos in this collection, finding them unexceptionally dull, cliché-ridden, and diffuse. His good reputation among his contemporaries seems to have lasted another couple hundred years: Dante mentions him four times in the *De vulgari* for instance. His fame, Pound suggests, may have been based on his tunes and the ultimate art of fitting a set of particular banalities perfectly to a lovely melody. The *Lums clartatz e verais* alba, easily his best work—it is quite short—EP has translated and somewhat improved.

"and the king of England Oc e No" : Oc e No is en Bertran's senhal for Richard Coeur de Lion, not for his father, Henry II. The young king is Henry's oldest son and Richard's brother.

"the young king was killed by a bolt from a crossbow in a castle of de Born's." : More confusion. It was Richard who was shot by a crossbowman from the walls of Châlus during the siege of that town on March 25, 1199: he died on April 6. Sixteen years earlier, having joined some of the rebel barons against his father, young Henry Plantagenet was returning north toward Brive from a raid on Rocamadour in the heat of June 1183. He fell ill of a fever and stopped at Martel, one of his own towns, resting at the house of a man called Étienne Fabri. He sent for his father, but received only a ring as token of his father's forgiveness. He died within a few days, aged 28. It is not recorded that Bertran was with him, but it is not unlikely. In any case, neither Martel nor Châlus belonged to de Born.

The meeting between Bertran and the old king is not otherwise recorded. However touching, it occurs in a context otherwise riddled with inaccuracies and cannot be trusted. The second vida confines itself to a general tracing of de Born's life, so makes no provable errors.

Lo coms m'a mandat e mogut

Clédat gives 1177 as a date for this piece. In that year, the count of Toulouse had to face a group of allies formed against him by the countess Ermengarde of Narbonne. But this war lasted several years, and the piece indicates clearly that the Aragonais were advancing on Toulouse. That, I think would make the best guess 1181. In that year "Alfons II advanced toward the Toulousin at the head of his troops, took a few castles, and came on to camp under the walls of the town without Raimon daring to show himself. He wreaked a little havoc in the suburbs and went on into Aquitaine." (*Histoire du Languedoc*). It should be added that Bernard IV of Comminges succeeded his father, Dodon, only in 1181.

Arramon Luc d'Esparro : Arramon is the Gascon form of Raimon. Esparron, canton d'Aurignac, Haute-Garonne.

Montagut : There's a Montaigut, canton of Grenade, 22 km. from Toulouse; and two others now spelled Montégut, in the cantons of Revel and Fousseret, further away, 44 and 60 km. respectively. In any case, the place-name is used for the rhyme.

"In the county meadow near the stone/steps" : (*peiro(n)*) At the bottom of the rue des Lois in Toulouse, a block from the Church of St.-Sernin and a half-block from the Faculté des Lettres, there's a Place du Peyrou. No one knows anymore where the county meadow was.

"And when we're all gathered together" : This is the beginning of stanza 5: I cut the fourth stanza. It says very little and, in English at least, slows up the poem. Let me give it here for the sake of completeness.

> *E seran i ab nos vengut*
> *Las poestatz e li baro*
> *E li plus honrat companho*
> *De·l mon e li plus mentaugut;*

Que per aver, que per somo,
Que per precs i seran vengut.

And gathered there with us there'll be
some powerful men and barons, the
most honored company in the world
and the most praised; (it doesn't matter)
if they come for gain or because the call
went out and they were asked,
they'll be there.

Alfons II of Aragon (1162-96) is not named, but the reference is plain.
Tarascon is in Provençe, and the whole political complexion of that area
was what was involved in this dispute between the count and the king.

William of Montarberon : disputed reading. Stimming has Mon Albeo
and refuses to guess which of Aragon's allies this might mean. Thomas
reads Montarbezo. Montauberon was a cloister near Montpellier and
Thomas sees the reference to Guillem VIII of Montpellier. It's a likely guess.
I only want to indicate that the reference is not clearly established.

Roger II, viscount of Béziers and Carcassonne (1167-1204).

Bernard-Aton VI, called The Younger; son of Bernard-Aton V, viscount
of Nîmes and Agde (1159-1214).

Peire de Lara of Narbonne, nephew and successor of Ermengarde,
countess of Narbonne.

The Count of Foix, Roger-Bernard II (1149-1188).

Bernard IV of Comminges (1181-1226).

Count Sancho, Alfons II's brother. He and Alfons were at Montpellier in
June 1181. Another reason why Guillem of Montpellier (above) is a good
guess.

Un sirventes cui motz no falh

The razos are by Uc de Saint Circ. I have given them where they exist.
As a rule, they are drawn directly from the text.

Diez and Stimming both give 1182 as the date of this sirventes. Richard had Périgueux under siege twice that spring, in April and in June.

Aimar : Adémar V, viscount of Limoges (1145-1199).

Richard is always Coeur de Lion, count of Poitou and duke of Aquitaine, old Oc e No, later to be the next Plantagenet king of England. He will turn up in all of these pieces except the *escondich*.

"If the king doesn't separate them" : the old king is Henry II of England, Eleanor of Aquitaine's second husband if you'd rather.

Guilhem de Gourdon (he was dead by 1195) was married to Alice de Turenne, sister of Maeut de Montanhac.

"The two viscounts" : it looks like he means Aimar and Richard here; is he demoting Richard? Guilhem must have insisted upon some extraordinary terms or assurances in the document mentioned and perhaps did not sign it because they were not forthcoming.

St. Leonard of the Limousin was the patron of prisoners. He broke these chains, see, and is depicted holding them.

Talairan : Elias V, Talairan, count of Périgord (1166-1205). The Talleyrand family produced a diplomat of genius some six centuries later.

"what the peacock tells the jackdaw" : Aesop #35. The peacock tells him to clear off; despite the elegance of his borrowed plummage he is still clearly a carrion-crow. Beat it.

Pois Ventadorns e Comborns ab Segur

Ventadorn : the Viscount was Ebles V; it is now the village of Moustier-Ventadour in the Corrèze.

Comborn : now a ruined castle near Orgnac (Corrèze); the viscount then was Archambaud V.

Segur : Ségur (Corrèze) was an important castle of the viscount of Limoges, Aimar V.

Turenne's viscount was Raimon II, b. 1143, d. 1191.

The lord of Montfort, Bernart de Cazenac, who was still alive in 1215. He was Alice of Turenne's second husband.

Gourdon and Périgord : *vide supra.*

Puy-Guillen, canton de Sigoulès (Dordogne).
Clérans, in the commune of Causse-de-Clérans, cant. de Lalinde, (Dordogne).
Grignol (Granhol), cant. de St.-Astier (Dordogne).
Saint-Astier (Dordogne), sort of the county seat.

"the counts of Angoulême" : Vulgrin III, the oldest son of count Guilhem IV of Angoulême, had died at the end of June 1181. He left only a daughter (Maeut) Mathilde, with whom Vulgrin's younger brothers (Elias, Guilhem, and Aimar) were disputing their father's heritage. Richard took up Mathilde's cause, and her uncles naturally were led to approach Philip-Augustus of France. De Born calls both Elias and Guilhem *Taliafer* (Iron-Cutter or Eisenhower, to translate that) a name all the counts of Angoulême carried at that time. The final stanza of this sirventes tells us that Taliafer (Elias?) did homage to Philip who recognized his legitimate claim, a fact (or rumor) which the chronicles seemed to not know or to ignore.

Milord the Waggoner : The young king Henry: see vida.

"the Gascons' boss" : Gaston VI, viscount of Béarn (1173-1215). Gavaudan is a small area whose center is Gavaret (Landes). In 1134 Peire, viscount of Gavaret, inherited Béarn. So in de Born's time both viscounts inhabited the person of Gaston VI.

Vezian II, Viscount of Lomagne (1173-1221). The name of Vezian is derived from the latin *Vidianus* AND IS STRICTLY meridional, not to be confused with Vivien (lat. *Bibianus*).

Bernard IV, Count of Armagnac (1160-1190).

Acs is the real name of Dax (Landes). Richard fought campaigns against Peire, viscount of Dax in 1177 and 1178.

Marsan was a district in Gascoigne which was in different viscounties at different times. At the time of the sirventes, it belonged to Centule, count of Bigorre, who had also fought Richard in 1177-78.

Talhaborc (Taillebourg) and Pons (Charente-Infériure) belonged to Jaufre of Rancon; both places taken by Richard in 1179.

Lusignan (Vienne), place of origin of an illustrious family, then belonging to Jaufre de Lusignan.

Tonnay-Charente (Charente-Infériure) whose lord was also called Jaufre (Geoffrey, Gottfried).

The lord of Mauléon (now Châtillon-sur-Sèvre, département des Deux-Sèvres) was Raoul, father of the celebrated Savaric de Mauléon.

Sivray : Civray (Vienne).

Toartz : Thouars (Deux-Sèvres). The viscount was Aimeric VII.

Mirabeau and Loudun (Vienne); L'Isle-Bouchard and Chinon (Indre-et-Loire). Clairvaux is now the parish of Scorbé-Clairvaux (Vienne). The construction of the fortress at Clairvaux was one of the complaints invoked by young Henry against his brother Richard at the end of 1182.

The young king: Henry ("Milord the Waggoner"), son of Henry II of England.

Matafelo : Fortress; now Mateflon in the commune of Seiches (Maine-et-Loire). That's up in Anjou.

Philip-Augustus of France succeeded his father, Louis VII, (Eleanor's first husband) on September 18, 1180. For all his seeming dependence on diplomacy and politics, Philip was the major opponent of the Plantagenet dynasty and Angevin empire, and persisted until it had destroyed itself from within, John Lackland and that mess in 1203, to which the French military successes of that year merely put the final hammer blows.

Charlemagne : Bertran was always bringing him up to needle the heir of the Capets.

Rassa, tan creis e monta e poja

"her, / who is clean empty of deceit" : Maeut de Montanhac.

"that plutocrat" : Richard.

Aigar e Maurin is a Provençal chanson de geste of which a fragment has come down to us.

"The viscount here" is Aimar of Limoges; the count is Richard.

"around Easter" : One is reminded constantly in de Born of the weather conditions in this sense: that winter weather stopped the hostilities, and that the wars began very predictably in the spring when the roads were passable.

Mariniers : the young king.

Golfier de la Tor : an in-law. His sister Agnes was married to en Bertran's brother, Constantin.

"my wicked Bel-Senhor" : Maeut again. "Say that he loved her, does it solve the riddle?"

Eu m'escondich, domna

[E: the escondich is a poem of self-justification.]

Montanhac, Montagnac, Montaignac, orthography again. Quercy is most frequently spelled Caersi, etc. The scribe's own pronunciation is often reflected in the mss.

The viscount of Comborn, as you have read already in other footnotes, was Archambaud V.

Guischart de Beljoc : Guichard V, lord of Beaujeu and Montpensier.

On the coblas of welcome for Guischarda, I must say they are the dullest of any writing attributed to de Born—mostly a string of the most arrant courtly compliment imaginable. I can't think what Maeut was jealous of:

perhaps the *Cel que chamja bo per malhor* for Miels-de-be (Guischarda again), though it sounds as if it were composed after the argument, and is anyway no great shakes as cansos go.

The *domna soisseubuda* : the "borrowed lady"; Ezra Pound has translated this piece, the *Dompna, pois de mi no·us cal*, beautifully—and again, there is no need to duplicate good work already done. For further speculations in the matter see Pound's poem *Near Périgord* which opens the *Lustra* section of his *Personae*.

The stanza I introduce by a gratuitous "By damn!" is thought to have been interpolated by (or from) the Monk of Montaudon, it being similar to a stanza of his in the *Fort m'enoia*. (p. 178 f.) The two men were contemporaries. I don't see that much similarity, besides I liked the way the strophe came out in English. Leave it in.

"badly-moulted . . . fidgety" : A bird in the process of moulting is very nervous and often kills the prey.

Greu m'es descendre charcol

Both Thomas and Clédat set this piece during the winter of 1186-87. Geoffrey of Brittany (Rassa), Richard's brother, died during the summer of 1186 in Paris, hob-nobbing with Philip-Augustus, the prime enemy of his house, over the reassignment of the Angevin lands after the young king's death. He was killed by a fall from his horse in the middle of a tournament. So I have set this piece after the Maeut-Guicharda business. The *Rassa tan creis* was addressed to Geoffrey.

"the lord of Molierna" : Henry II of England. Mouliherne (Mainte-et-Loire) is a town in Anjou. Old Henry Fitz-Empress was the son of Geoffrey Plantagenet, count of Anjou.

"that lord who has Bordeaux" : Richard. He is compared to a grinding stone, and the barons to a sword with an edge which refuses, despite a good honing down, to cut worth a damn.

Berlais de Mosterol : an Angevin lord with a fighting reputation, notably against Henry I of England. He has left his name in its French version, Montreuil, to an end-of-the-line stop on the Paris Metro.

Guilhem de Monmaurel : one of Guillem IX's captains. He died in the Pyrenees during a campaign into Spain in 1122.

Mirandol is a castle in the community of Martel (Lot), the most important town in Turenne; Creysse is nearby. Sufficient for Stimming and Thomas to say that the lord of Mirandol is Raimon II, viscount of Turenne.

Benauges : a district in the old Bordelais. The ms. has Beirmes.

Cognac : (Charente-Inférieure); and Mirabeau (Vienne).

Chartres : probably Chastres near Cognac, nothing to do with the cathedral town.

St.-Jean d'Angely (Charente-Inférieure).

Botenan : Boutavant, the castle of the Vexin, today in the Oise.

Merlin : Someone suggests an allusion to some prophecy of Merlin's in some romance of which we have no trace. Sure.

"who praises himself in his singing" : Alfons II of Aragon was himself a troubadour. Bertran is constantly making cracks at him. I remember reading somewhere that after leaving the walls of Toulouse intact in 1181, Alfons came up into Aquitaine and helped Richard attack Altafort in 1182. That would have been enough reason.

"I turned toward where the tooth hurts me" : There was likely a popular proverb behind this idea. Essentially the same metaphor occurs as early as Marcabru (c. 1130-48) and as late as Folquet de Marseille (c. 1180-95).

"toward her" : Maeut again, most likely.

un austor tercel : a tercel-hawk, today a tiercelet.

Tristan : the senhal occurs nowhere else in de Born. Bernart de Ventadorn used it, presumably with Eleanor of Aquitaine. Guess here: Tibor de Montausier.

far cinc e terna : gambling terms. The commentators say from a lottery game, something called tric-trac? Sounds to me like dice. *Terna* could

mean a triple as well as a three. In any case, I'd guess it was a winning combination, comparable, perhaps, to the daily-double.

No puosc mudar un chantar non esparga

"Since Oc e No has set the fire" : After taking the cross at Gisors with his
father, with Philip-Augustus, with the counts of Flanders and of Blois and
many other powerful nobles, in the spring of 1187, Richard accompanied
his father to Le Mans, then headed south to impose the Truce of God in
Poitou and the Limousin, where the barons were in revolt as usual. Not
stopping with that, he proceeded south through the Limousin and the Auvergne to Launguedoc and Toulouse itself. He took seventeen or eighteen
castles from the count of Toulouse, as well as the towns of Cahors and
Moissac, and was ravaging the countryside around the city. Raimon V
appealed to the French king as his overlord, and by May or June 1188,
there were reports that Philip, breaking the vow he'd made at Gisors, had
struck into Berry and had taken Châteauroux and other castles. That
would place this sirventes in the spring or summer of 1188.

"the two kings" : In July 1188 the old king Henry crossed the Channel
from Portsea to Barfleur with his crusade recruits from England and Wales
and met Philip-Augustus under the great elm on the banks of the Epte near
Gisors, the traditional meeting place of the kings of France and the dukes
of Normandy. The various proposals were coming to nothing and a scrap
developed between the troops. The French troops turned with fury on the
elm and chopped it down with axes and swords. When the great landmark
had fallen, Henry renounced his vassal's allegiance, invaded French lands,
took the city of Mantes and ravaged the lands about it.

Rancon and Lusignan : baronies in the Limousin and Poitou.

Rouen is located at a loop of the Seine with a cliff rising close behind it,
and very difficult of attack. The siege of Rouen was conducted by Louis
VII, Philip's father, during the first three weeks of August 1174. The Norman capital did not fall.

The chanson de geste *Guiteclin* is concerned with Charlemagne's conquest of Saxony; another epic poem, *Aspremont*, recounts his conquest of
Apulia and that part of Italy.

"one whom no man had found frank" : possibly meaning Philip; but my

309

guess here is Raimon V, count of Toulouse, who appealed to the king of the Franks for aid, *i.e.*, who would have thought him a Frenchman?

Chinon : the treasure castle of the Angevins in the Touraine. Richard is said to have pillaged it in 1187, not counting on an spontaneous access of generosity on his father's part. Henry II died there July 6, 1189. After his burial in an abbey at Fontevrault, Richard hurried off to Chinon.

"for her who does not wish to keep me" : Maeut, probably.

Treignac : The county seat of Corrèze in the Limousin. No one guesses at who Roger might be. *omba, om,* and *esta* are the rhymes in lines 4, 5, and 8 of each stanza of the sirventes.

Mei sirventes : a sirventes usually runs six or seven strophes. This one runs three-and-a-half.

Alfons VII of Castile (1158-1214). There is no record of such a clash coming off. Clédat puts the date of this sirventes at 1195. That was a fairly quiet year, devoted chiefly to negotiations and bargaining. The year before was a different matter. In May of 1194 Richard had chased Phillipe-Auguste out of Normandy and swept down the Loire recovering castles surrendered by John during Richard's captivity as well as Loches and Châteaudun, almost capturing Philip himself. Among the spoils taken in the rout were charters of Breton, Angevin, and Poitevin barons who were in collusion with Philip. The Plantagenet lands were honeycombed with traitors and Richard had the list.

If en Bertrans were on Richard's side this time, and he was sometimes, the sirventes may have been a message to tell Richard that the count of Angoulême and Jaufre de Rancon had sent to Castile for aid. If de Born were with the rebels such news or rumor would have been sheer bluff. In any case, nothing slowed Richard down. In July 1194 he descended upon the rebel castles, burning and devastating. Within three weeks he had taken the castles and all the territory of Jaufre de Rancon in the Charente valley, and the city of Angoulême as well. In Richard's first contest after his return from captivity, he had shown that he had not lost his taste for battle. He had driven the king of France back to the Île and overrun the strongholds of the rebels within his own borders. It was a busy summer, color it red.

Be·m platz lo gais temps de pascor

No date can be assigned to this piece in praise of war, perhaps the most famous of de Born's sirventes. Its savage description of the joys of battle is the major source for Pound's *Sestina Altaforte*, and Pound's version of the tornada appears a number of times in *The Cantos*.

THE MONK OF MONTAUDON

EDITOR'S NOTES

VIDA

Montaudon has been identified as a Benedictine monastery in the Auvergne. The Monk, according to Bergin and Hill (I. 137), was born Pierre de Vic.

King Amfos of Aragon is Alfonso II of Aragon.

L'autrier fuy en paradis

"...that king who has Oléron" is Richard Coeur de Lion; Oléron is an island off the southwest coast of France.

Fort m'enoia, so auzes dir

The *enueg* is a poem of vexation, of *annoy*ance, a kind of opposite number to the *plazer*, for an example of which see above, the Monk's *Molt me platz deportz e gaieza*.

Pois Peire d'Alvernhe a chantat

After Peire d'Alvernhe's sirventes *Chantarai d'aquestz trobadors*, for which see above, pp. 85-87.

The Viscount of Sant Antonin is Raimon Jordan. He, along with Gaucelm Faidit, Arnaut Daniel, and Peire Vidal, would be known to readers of this volume. The others range from the fairly well-known, such as en Folque (Folquet de Marseilla), to mere names like en Tremolet, whose work is lost. See Bergin and Hill, II. 48-50.

The last three stanzas are generally considered to be unauthentic. In any case, Caussada is near Montaudon and Lobeat has never been identified; who en Bernat was doesn't seem very important under the circumstances.

GUILHEM DE CABESTANH

EDITOR'S NOTES

VIDA

The translation of this vida was done by the editor.

The legend of the lover's eaten heart had a wide currency in medieval literature. Ezra Pound incorporated it—with delicate cinematic concision—into *Canto IV:*

> "It is Cabestanh's heart in the dish."
> "It is Cabestanh's heart in the dish?
> "No other taste shall change this."
> And she went toward the window,
>   the slim white stone bar
> Making a double arch;
> Firm even fingers held to the firm pale stone;
> Swung for a moment,
>   and the wind out of Rhodez
> Caught in the full of her sleeve.

GAUCELM FAIDIT ET AL

EDITOR'S NOTES

VIDA

The last sentence does not belong to the Provençal vida; Blackburn has added it—in emulation of a convention common in the vidas and razos—as a lead into the dawn-song he has selected from Gaucelm's poems.

312

Partimen

Similar to the *tenso*, the *partimen*, also called *joc partit*, is a debate poem in which a poet suggests a choice of argument to one or more colleagues and accepts the rejected choice for himself. Readers familiar with the works of Boccaccio and Chaucer will recognize that the type of question treated in this partimen is a *demande d'amour*.

Savaric de Mauleon was a rich and handsome baron of Poitiers who played in tournaments, made love to the ladies, and composed songs. He fought against the King of France—all this according to his vida. King John of England gave him English peerage as a reward for his support.

According to his brief vida, Uc de la Bacalaria (La Bachélerie, near Uzerche) was a joglar who also made some good poems.

Mos-Garda-Cors means she-who-keeps-my-heart.

Lady Marie, without a doubt, refers to Maria of Ventadorn (born c. 1165), one of the women troubadours. She was also well-known as a patron of troubadours, her husband being Ebles V of Ventadorn, the great-grandson of Ebles II, the contemporary of Guillem IX. The court at Venta-dorn would have been an ideal place, practically or rhetorically, to refe the question.

Guillema is, of course, mentioned in Gaucelm's vida; Benauges was th chief fortress of the viscounty of the same name in present-day Gironde

AIMERIC DE PEGUILHAN

EDITOR'S NOTES

VIDA

King Alfons of Castile is Alfonso VIII.
"Catharists" is Blackburn's translation, here and elsewhere, of *li bon home*. See above, the note to Peire d'Alvernhe's vida, p. 283.

Mantas vetz sui enqueritz

Tornada: the Marquis William Malaspina was one of Aimeric's favorite patrons. The Este family was also one of his patrons during his stay in northern Italy.

Can que·m fezes vers ni canso

Flabel (or *fablel*) derives from the Latin *fabula*. As Aimeric says in the second line, it is a poem without tune or melody—"moz senes so."

"...there to la Marca to en Sordel" refers to the Italian troubadour Sordello in the province of Le Marche.

GAVAUDAN

EDITOR'S NOTES

There is no surviving biographical evidence of Gavaudan's career except for his eleven extant poems.

Lo vers dech far

King Anfos is probably Alfonso VIII of Castile.

PONS DE CAPDUEILL

EDITOR'S NOTES

Qui per nesci cuidar

"...if she wants to pardon me/with both hands," refers to a gesture from a feudal lord towards his vassal in which the placing of both of the

314

lord's hands around the right hand of the vassal symbolized acceptance or forgiveness.

Tristan and Iseult were the most famous lovers of medieval romance.

CADENET

EDITOR'S NOTE

Excellent background reading for the study of the *alba* is provided by Jonathan Saville, *The Medieval Erotic Alba* (New York, 1972). Saville's third chapter, "The Watchman and the Lady," is especially enlightening; Cadenet's poem is specifically discussed on pp. 114-120.

SORDELLO

EDITOR'S NOTES

VIDAS

Cunizza da Romano's soul appears in Dante's *Paradiso* IX. 8-10. The count of Provence is Raymond Bérenger IV.

Planher vuelh en Blacatz en aquest leugier so

This most famous of Sordello's poems, which provided Dante with the basis for his noble characterization of the Mantuan troubadour in *Purgatorio* VI-VII, is generally viewed as a combination of the planh and the sirventes.

En Blacatz, the subject of the funeral lament and the standard for the moral attack, was a Provençal nobleman (a vassal of Count Raymond Bérenger IV) and a patron of numerous troubadours, including Sordello. He died between 1235-39.

The Roman Emperor refers to Frederick II of Sicily, who for many years fought the Pope and the League of Milan.

The King of Castile should refer to Louis IX (Saint Louis) of France, whose mother, Blanche of Castile, influenced to claim the throne of Castile. However, in a rare lapse, Blackburn has erroneously conflated the poem's two different references to Castile: he probably meant Ferdinand III of Castile and Lèón, who is referred to in the original a few lines later. Both Ferdinand and Louis IX were dominated by their mothers, and Louis did lay claim to Castile; hence, their confusion.

The King of England is Henry III. He failed to regain the lands his father, John Lackland, lost to France.

The King of Aragon refers to James I, the cousin of Count Raymond Bérenger IV; James and the Count of Provence failed to put down a revolt by the city of Marseille. Aveyron is the viscounty of Milhau, which James claimed.

The King of Navarre refers to Thibaut IV of Champagne, who inherited the throne of Navarre in 1234 through his mother, Blanche. He was not particularly appreciated there, but for us he remains a fairly important medieval French poet. See Goldin, *Lyrics of the Troubadours and Trouvères*, pp. 443-81, for an informative introduction and an ample selection of his work.

The Count of Toulouse is Raymond VII. At the Treaty of Meaux in 1229, he lost most of his lands to the King of France.

The Count of Provence, of course, is Raymond Bérenger.

Fair Healer is a senhal which most editors agree stands for Guida of Rodez.

Robert Browning and Ezra Pound, as well as Dante, thought Sordello worth writing about.

AIMERIC DE BELENOI

EDITOR'S NOTE

Nulhs hom no pot cumplir

"...the lovely Eleanor" is probably a senhal for the lady from Gascoigne named Gentils de Rius mentioned in the vida. Gentils de Rius is never named in any of Aimeric's poems.

BERNART ARNAUT MONCUC

EDITOR'S NOTES

Moncuc is a town in Quercy.

Er quan li rozier

Tarzana has not been satisfactorily identified by anyone.

Balaguier is the town of Balaguer in northern Spain.

"The valorous king" refers to Pedro II of Aragon, who came to help defend the South (and in his own interests) during the Albigensian Crusade; he was killed by the forces of Simon de Monfort at the Battle of Muret on September 12, 1213, which date clearly serves as *terminus ad quem* for the composition of the poem.

The English king refers to King John.

"GUIANA!" is another name for the ducy of Aquitaine and is used here as a battlecry.

"And I shall be the first the count/decorates for valor" refers to Count Raymond VI of Toulouse, Bernart's lord.

Senher means lord or master and refers here to Bernart's lady.

MONTANHAGOL

EDITOR'S NOTES

Del tot vey remaner valor

"...clerks and frères prêcheurs" refers to the clergy and to the Dominican Order, which administered the Inquisition in the South.

"The valiant count" refers to Raymond VI of Toulouse.

PEIRE CARDENAL

EDITOR'S NOTES

VIDA

Jacme of Aragon is James I (1213-76).

Miquel de la Tor, according to Bergin and Hill, II. 68, was himself the author of a now lost collection of troubadour poems.

Tan son valen nostre vezi

A marabotin is a Moorish coin of gold or silver.

Trebellius refers to the Roman consul who first proposed the function and office of what we would describe today as fiduciary.

Li clerc si fan pastor

"...Alengri the wolf" refers to Ysengrimus, the wolf in the medieval beast epic.

The Alcays and Almassors are Arab chiefs and sultans.

Frederick refers to Frederick II of Sicily. His own father-in-law, who attacked him—unsuccessfully—in 1229, is the "one" mentioned in the next lines.

Tos temps azir falsetat et enjan

A tornes is a coin of Tours.

Tartarassa ni voutor

Malamen means badly, through evil practices.

PEDRO III OF ARAGON ET AL

EDITOR'S NOTES

Peire Salvatg' en greu pessar

The historical background of these coblas (strophes) was shaped by the War of the Sicilian Vespers through which Peter (Pedro) the Great of Aragon thwarted the ambitions of Charles Anjou; the war, which began in 1282 and lasted for twenty years, involved Sicily—with Peter III of Aragon as its new king—against the Angevins, the Papacy, and sometimes France. It is no wonder that in the third line of his initial strophe Pedro mentions "the heavy smell/of *fleur de lis.*"

"And now my nephew would like to change/sides," refers to the fact that Charles was Pedro's sister's son.

"...from here to Monmelian" refers to a town in Savoie, i.e., all the way to southeastern France.

"Montjoi" is the famous battlecry of the French in *La Chanson de Roland* and thus is apt for the men of the Count of Foix.

"'*Oil* and *Nenil*' in place of '*Oc* and *No*'!" refers to the different languages of Old French and Old Provençal, the four italicized words being the affirmative and negative particles in each tongue.

"...down past Canigou" refers to a mountain in the eastern Pyrenees.

"But tell me, can all that be done/without the lion?", i.e., without the help of the King of León and Castile.

Castelbon is a valley and viscounty in Catalonia, Spain.

GIRAUT RIQUIER

Giraut Riquier, born around 1230, composed c. 1254-1282, and returned to France around 1280, is almost the last of the troubadours. Giraut is best known, perhaps, for a series of six pastorelas, which seem to be written between 1260-1282, in which he tackles the same shepherdess with the same dismal results each time. The group, in that sense, constitutes a novela, for in the last piece he is attempting the virtue of the shepherdess' daughter, who apparently has as stinging a tongue as her mother. Those pieces are not included here. I translated the whole package but in the end could not get versions which satisfied me. I'm sorry. So you'll do without. Chaucer might have done a good job of translating them, had he known the pieces. You get the idea.

Since Mossen Girautz has had no one to write his vida, let me compose one here and now in his honor.

VIDA

Giraut Riquier was from Narbonne, in the lands of the count of Toulouse. And he was of great worth and a handsome man in his person. He had a good voice and knew trobar well, and was well-taught in letters.

320

And when the Inquisition had the power in Narbonne, he went down into Spain to the court of Alfons X of Castile. And there the king gave him a fine welcome, as did all the fine ladies and valiant barons of Spain. And he stayed there for a long while (10 years or so), and fell in love with a noble lady of that court, and made many good cansos for her. And he called her in his songs Belh Deport.

Once he addressed a *supplicatio* to King Alfons, to the effect that a more severe distinction be made and proclaimed between joglars and troubadours, because the use of the terms had grown so slack in application. For often a joglar, some low fellow of no worth, with a doubtful character and no talent, would be called by the name troubadour, while a troubadour of great worth and genius would be called a joglar, and the one the other. Also he asked that the troubadours of greatest worth be called by the title Doctor of Trobar, to honor them as greatly as they deserved, for the craft had fallen that much into neglect. And the king granted it to him.

And Giraut Riquier composed in many modes: cansos, sirventes, epistolas, tensos, albas, serenas, and pastorelas. And when he wrote down his songs, many times he wrote down also the date of composition and the kind of piece it was, for he was a very scrupulous man with great care for the old traditions. And he stayed for a long time in the court of Castile, and was held in great honor by the king and the great nobles and the Catharist refugees, many of whom had been of noble birth with great lands in their own country.

Afterward he went back into Provence, and stayed with Enric (II) count of Rodez, who was a noble, generous, and open-handed baron. There were other troubadours at that court, and he stayed there a long time. And here was written down one of his songs, as you have heard.

SELECTED BIBLIOGRAPHY

Obviously, this is a very selective list, with criticism confined mainly to works in English. I have included all of the works Blackburn mentions (by author) in his notes, but I do not claim to have identified all of the studies and texts he may have consulted or used in the preparation of his translations and notes. My own indebtednesses, more specifically indicated in my notes, are acknowledged generally here.

The abbreviation CFMA stands for *Classiques Français du Moyen Âge*.

Anglade, Joseph, ed. *Les poésies de Peire Vidal*, 2nd ed., CFMA 11. Paris, 1966.

Bartsch, Karl, ed. *Chrestomathie provençale*, 6th ed., rev. Eduard Koschwitz. Marburg, 1904.

Ballard, Jean et al., eds. *Cahiers de Sud*, XX (1942), numéro spécial: "Le Génie d'Oc et l'Homme Méditerranéen."

Bergin, Thomas G. and R. T. Hill, eds. *Anthology of the Provençal Troubadours*. 1st ed. New Haven, 1941. 2nd ed., 2 vols. New Haven and London, 1973.

Blackburn, Paul. "Proensa: A Reading at Long Island University, Brooklyn Center," December 14, 1965: on tape.

Bogin, Meg. *The Women Troubadours*. New York, 1976.

323

Boutière, Jean and A. -H. Schutz, eds. *Biographies des troubadours.* Toulouse and Paris, 1950. 2nd ed., 1964.

Dejeanne, J. -M. -L., ed. *Poésies complète du troubadour Marcabru.* Toulouse, 1909, reprinted New York, 1971.

Diez, Friedrich. *Leben und Werke der Troubadours.* Leipzig, 1882, reprinted Amsterdam, 1965.

———. *Die Poesie der Troubadours.* Leipzig, 1883.

Dronke, Peter. *Medieval Latin and the Rise of European Love-Lyric.* 2 vols. Oxford, 1965-1966.

———. *The Medieval Lyric.* New York, 1968.

Ferrante, Joan M. and George D. Economou, eds. *In Pursuit of Perfection: Courtly Love in Medieval Literature.* Port Washington, N.Y. and London, 1975.

Goldin, Frederick. *The Mirror of Narcissus in the Courtly Love Lyric.* Ithaca, 1967.

———. *Lyrics of the Troubadours and Trouvères.* New York, 1973.

Hoepffner, Ernest. *Les troubadours dans leur vie et dans leur oeuvres.* Paris, 1955.

———. *Le troubadour Peire Vidal.* Paris, 1961.

Jeanroy, Alfred. *La poésie lyrique des troubadours.* Toulouse and Paris, 1934.

———, ed. *Les chansons de Jaufré Rudel,* 2nd ed. CFMA 15, Paris, 1965.

———. *Les Origines de la poésie lyrique en France au moyen-âge,* 4th ed. Paris, 1965.

———, ed. *Les poésies de Cercamon.* CFMA 27. Paris, 1966.

———. ed. *Les chansons de Guillaume IX,* 2nd ed. CFMA 9. Paris, 1967.

Klein, Karen W. *The Partisan Voice: A Study of the Political Lyric in France and Germany, 1180-1230.* The Hague and Paris, 1971.

Jackson. W. T. H. *The Literature of the Middle Ages.* New York, 1960.

Lavaud, René, ed. *Peire Cardenal.* Toulouse, 1957.

Lewis, C. S. *The Allegory of Love.* Oxford, 1936.

Marshall, J. H., ed. *The Razos de Trobar of Raimon Vidal and Associated Texts.* London, 1972.

Nelli, René. *L'Erotique des troubadours.* Toulouse, 1963.

Newman, F. X., ed. *The Meaning of Courtly Love.* Albany, 1968.

Pillet, A. and H. Carstens. *Bibliographie der Troubadours.* Halle/Saale, 1933.

Press, Alan P. *Anthology of Troubadour Lyric Poetry.* Austin, 1971.

Previté-Orton, C. W. *The Shorter Cambridge Medieval History,* 2 vols. Cambridge, 1971.

Saville, Jonathan. *The Medieval Erotic Alba: Structure as Meaning.* New York, 1972.

Stróński, S. *Le troubadour Folquet de Marseille.* Cracow, 1910.

Stimming, A., ed. *Bertran de Born, Sein Leben und seine Werke.* Halle, 1879.

Topsfield, L. T. *Troubadours and Love.* Cambridge, 1975.

van der Werf, Hendrik. *The Chansons of the Troubadours and Trouvères: A Study of the Melodies and their Relation to the Poems,* Utrecht, 1972.

Valency, Maurice. *In Praise of Love.* New York, 1958.

Wilhelm, James J. *The Cruelest Month.* New Haven, 1965.

———. *Seven Troubadours, The Creators of Modern Verse.* University Park and London, 1970.

Wiacek, Wilhelmina M. *Lexique des noms géographiques et ethniques dans les poésies des troubadours des XIIe et XIIIe siècles.* Paris, 1968.

Zingarelli, Nicola. *Intorno a due trovatori in Italia.* Florence, 1899.

ADDITIONAL REFERENCES

Appel, Carl, ed. *Provenzalische Chrestomathie,* 6th ed. Leipzig, 1930.

Bartholomaeis, Vincenzo de. *Poesi provenzali storiche relative all'Italia,* 2 vols. Rome, 1931.

Canello, U. A. *La Vita e le opere del trovatore Arnaldo Daniello.* Halle, 1883.

Clédat, L. *Du Rôle historique de Bertran de Born.* Paris, 1879.

Crescini, Vincenzo. *Manuale per l'avviamento agli studi provenzali,* 3d ed. Milan, 1926.

Thomas, Antoine, ed. *Poésies complète de Bertran de Born.* Toulouse, 1888.

Wolff, P. *Histoire du Languedoc.* Toulouse, 1967.